Don't Let Your EMOTIONS Run Your Life

How Dialectical Behavior Therapy Can Put You in Control

SCOTT E. SPRADLIN, MA

NEW HARBINGER PUBLICATIONS, INC.

Publisher's Note

This publication is designed to provide accurate and authoritative information in regard to the subject matter covered. It is sold with the understanding that the publisher is not engaged in rendering psychological, financial, legal, or other professional services. If expert assistance or counseling is needed, the services of a competent professional should be sought.

To all of my DBT clients past and present
who have been so gracious as to let me participate
in their struggles for life and their journeys toward healing.

Contents

PART III
Reducing Blocks to Emotion Regulation

PART IV
Leading an Emotionally Skillful Life

Acknowledgments

A number of people have had a hand in this book coming to be—some directly, others indirectly. I appreciate and thank Patrick Fanning and Matthew McKay of New Harbinger Press for inviting me to do this project. Also at New Harbinger I must thank Tesilya Hanauer and Heather Mitchener for "editorial motivation," and walking with me through this process. They made this experience enjoyable and worthwhile. To William Rodarmor, I truly appreciate his wit, focus, and skill. He did a tremendous job of streamlining mangled sentences and paragraphs and saved the public from inane academic jargon and charts.

It was Brad Hubert and Greg Mulkey, then of Luke-Dorf, Inc., who first sent me to train in dialectical behavior therapy (DBT). This led me to Soonie Kim, Ph.D., who provided an excellent introduction to DBT principles and practices, and who brought me into the DBT fold, as it were, by inviting me to become a member of the Portland DBT Program. The team at Portland DBT demonstrated phenomenological empathy, compassion, and fallibility. Particularly Alice Rose, LCSW, who mentored me in leading skills-training groups (to this day I mimic you when I lead groups). It was a great honor to work with true experts.

Immeasurable gratitude goes to Marsha Linehan, Linda Dimeff, and Kelly Koerner of Behavioral Technology Transfer Group—the DBT trinity, in my mind. The Seattle intensive was like boot camp for DBT therapists. This training increased my theoretical knowledge of borderline personality disorder (BPD) and DBT, but most importantly, their personal commitment to the clients we treat renewed my compassion, confidence, and sense of mission in treating borderline individuals. Many of these clients not only survive because of DBT but are also thriving beyond their own expectations. If not for Marsha's team and research, many of us would still be at a loss for how help our borderline clients. I hope this workbook does justice to DBT, and will be a usable tool for clients and practitioners.

It was at the Portland Providence Medical Center's Crisis Triage Center (CTC), that my limits and creativity were stretched during my stint as "Captain Midnight," adapting DBT to crisis calls on the graveyard shift. My time there has influenced my practice, especially with respect to teaching clients skills for collaborating with crisis service providers. The clinical and medical staff showed hope in the face of despair and helped me to see our work as a healing art. While at the CTC, I'm grateful to have become friends with Jane Erickson, Deb Roth, and Ellen Barker (aka "Encarta") and for their encouragement on the workbook as well as their general concern for Captain Midnight. Likewise for Marianne Irish for creative friendship and her love of poetry, and Elyce Benham, who was the Sculley to my Mulder and with whom I shared the overnights.

I simply must thank all of the café owners and baristas who tolerated me loitering with my laptop during this process. In Portland, Oregon, I thank the Starbucks crew at 45th & Glisan where I could write on break from my shifts at Providence Hospital. I especially thank John Asparro and Valerie Dianna of True Brew Café in Southeast Portland for the most affordable and delicious lattes ever. In Wichita, Kansas, I thank Amy Clarke, an Oregon transplant and proprietor of the Bean Scene, and the kind people at Watermark Books & Cafe.

My good friend Rebecca Campbell, doctoral candidate in neuroendocrinology at Oregon Health Science University provided several informal consultations about brain functions, and the napkin diagram of the hypothalamus. Blessings to you and Andrew as you move to New Zealand. T. J. Civis is a creative friend and filmmaker who also encouraged me by working on his own projects and through our short-lived writers group.

Finally, I thank my psychologist wife, Jill, for her encouragement to complete this project and all the free therapy. It was her attendance at George Fox University that led us to Portland and resulted in my involvement in DBT, and so, in a manner of thinking, this project is perhaps ultimately thanks to her.

Introduction

The principles and techniques presented in this workbook derive from my training and experience as a practitioner of dialectical behavior therapy (DBT), which was developed by Marsha Linehan and her colleagues at the University of Washington. DBT has garnered accolades from professionals and recipients of therapy for its effectiveness in treating borderline personality disorder (BPD).

People affected by BPD suffer quick, intense emotional spikes, which send them reeling into emotional dysregulation. It can take borderlines a long time to recover from these spikes and return to their normal mood or emotional "baseline." The experience has been described as "heating up like a microwave oven but cooling down like a conventional one." It's as though the emotions take over, and once they do, it takes a while before the people are back in control. And while these people are cooling off, they're even more vulnerable to the next trigger.

People diagnosed with BPD are emotionally sensitive, and find themselves being overly emotional, but they aren't the only ones who have trouble regulating their emotions—we all do. There have probably been times in each of our lives when we can remember not being in our "right mind," and we've all heard of crimes of passion committed in the heat of a moment.

There's a wide spectrum of emotional sensitivity, and it varies from one person to another. Some people oscillate between over-control and over-expression. Others stuff or hide their emotions for months before they finally blow their stack and "stand up for themselves" through overly aggressive behaviors. All of this is to say that you don't need to be formally diagnosed with an emotional disorder to benefit from this book. You may be a person who has been formally diagnosed and be in treatment, but that's not a requirement. The book can help you to better understand your emotions, and to see that they play an important role in your life—aside from torturing you. It may also help reduce your vulnerability to being overly emotional, and decrease self-defeating beliefs, thoughts, and judgments about yourself.

You might say this is a book for increasing your emotional intelligence. It addresses factors such as physiology, the nature of emotion, diet, relationships, skills for cooling down, and ways to understand how to experience your emotions with less self-judgment.

As we get underway, I want to acknowledge that as a DBT practitioner, much of the material here is based on the ideas of Marsha Linehan and her colleagues at the University of Washington, and Linehan's published material in her *Cognitive-Behavioral Treatment of Borderline Personality Disorder* (1993a) and her *Skills Training Manual for Treating Borderline Personality Disorder* (1993b). I also draw from the intensive training I received through the Behavioral Technology Transfer Group (BTTG) in Seattle. In my own work as a therapist and in writing this workbook, I have been inspired not only by Marsha Linehan and the DBT model, but also by the courage shown by so many of my clients in their struggle to integrate DBT into their lives, becoming more skillful as they build lives worth living. I hope this work will reflect all of these qualities in a friendly and ultimately effective tool for you, the reader.

Assumptions about the Reader

In DBT we have a whole set of assumptions that we like to make and keep explicit throughout treatment. These assumptions guide our work as therapists, and they guide the hard work that our clients engage in. At this point, I want to put forth the six assumptions that I'm making about you, the reader. I hope that in time you will come to adopt them as your own.

1. At present, you are doing the very best that you can in dealing with your emotions.

2. You want to do better and be more skillful in dealing with your emotions.

3. You need to do better, try harder, and be more motivated to change.

4. You may not have created all of your own problems, but you have to solve them anyway.

5. You are currently unsatisfied with the way in which you deal with your emotions.

6. You must learn new emotion skills and behaviors in all relevant contexts.

Unpacking the Assumptions

Let's go through each of those assumptions, and see how they might apply to your special circumstances.

1. At present, you are doing the very best that you can in dealing with your emotions.

This may come as a surprise to you. On the one hand you might think, "If this is the best I can do, then buddy, I am in some very deep water." On the other hand you might be thinking, "If this is the best I can do with my emotions, then I'm lazy, stupid, or crazy." If you take either one of these positions you may be beset with a storm of internalized invalidations, your "old tapes," or be too in touch with your inner critic. This first assumption is actually saying that, given your life history, your physiology, and your current level of skillfulness, you really are doing the best that you can. We all are doing the best that we can. Can you do better? Yes, of course—but that comes next.

Think for a moment about how your parents modeled emotional expression and control for you. Did they deride emotion, or did they acknowledge your communication of emotion as valid and accurate? Did they express their emotions violently, or did they keep them stuffed up inside? These factors make a huge difference in how we experience, control, and express emotion, and these factors affect all of us. If you swear and throw things whenever you lose your keys, chances are that your parents did the same thing. That's modeling. And if every time you throw something out of anger, you then immediately feel your arousal level go down and get a sense of relief, that relief will work as a reinforcer. That in turn will strengthen your angry-throwing-behaviors for future repeats, so you'll probably do it again, even though it violates your values. But you might look at throwing something angrily as a skill, because it does help you eventually regulate your emotions. You're simply using what you know.

PARENTS

MODELING

REINFORCE

Assumptions can really get us going. They can build hope or they can bring our best efforts to a screeching halt. For now, as you read and work your way through this book, I ask that you adopt this first assumption on the list, at least pragmatically. Give it the old college try, try it on, take it for a spin. See whether or not it makes a difference. It requires both commitment and faith, like the rest of the assumptions. Keep these assumptions in front of you as much as possible, especially if you find your old assumptions coming back, threatening your progress. You don't have to marry them now, but you may come to love them enough that you will want to later.

2. You want to do better and be more skillful in dealing with your emotions.

Well, doesn't this stand to reason? You want to get better, do better, be better, and that's why you're reading this workbook. It will aid you in your quest to be more emotionally balanced. I want this assumption to reinforce your desire to increase that sense of balance. That's why we're explicitly stating it here. If you hear the dire voices of doubt telling you that you're lazy or lack motivation, come back to this assumption to remind yourself that you're not lazy—you just want to change.

3. You need to do better, try harder, and be more motivated to change.

We already said that you are doing the best that you can, yet now we are saying you can do better. What's that about? This is one of those dialectical, both/and tensions that can alert us to all-or-nothing thinking. While some people may assume that the best one is doing is as good as it gets, and that's that, DBT says you're doing the best you can *and* you can do better. You haven't reached your absolute limit of personal growth.

4. You may not have created all of your own problems, but you have to solve them anyway.

In my work as a DBT skills group facilitator, this is the one assumption above the others that receives the most "Amens!" It gets approval since it says that not all of your problems are your fault. But amid the unbridled enthusiasm, I have to remind my groups to the warning light in *"may* not have," and of course the whole second clause in the sentence: "but you have to solve them anyway." That one's a bummer—but it's not an absolute bummer.

This assumption contains two blessings. One, it acknowledges that many of your problems have been given to you by others, so not everything is your fault. See, you're just not that bad. Two, in saying that you have to solve these problems, this assumption is a vote for your ability to actually solve them. So the second blessing is a belief in your capacity to learn, to grow, to change, to do differently. You can do it. The reality is, that whenever you have a problem, it's a problem to be solved, and most likely can be solved in some way. And if it's *your* problem, then you do have to solve it.

5. You are currently unsatisfied with the way in which you deal with your emotions.

Again, I assume that if you're working through this book, you're dissatisfied with the state of your emotional life. For example, you may have the experience of either being out of touch with your emotions, or having your emotions run you into impulsive behaviors or a sense of suffering and chaos. Either way, you're probably unsatisfied with that way of being.

6. You must learn new emotion skills and behaviors in all relevant contexts.

It isn't enough to feel confident when you're at home with your goldfish, or to feel happy while watching a TV sitcom about beautiful friendships. You need to change some of your emotional responses in all contexts in which you operate. If you're having trouble with anger at work, you'll need to work at non-angry, relaxed, and kind behaviors there—not just on the drive home following an outburst that you may deeply regret. If you experience tremendous shame speaking in front of others, you'll need to speak without that shame at home, in church, at work, the pub, the school board meeting, wherever you need or want to freely engage with others.

Final Words about the Assumptions

The six assumptions I listed above are reminders for you to turn to whenever you find yourself getting discouraged. Like beacons, they help guide you back to your original course whenever you drift into hopelessness or fatigue, or encounter discouraging and hurtful persons. The assumptions keep you alerted to your wise mind values and goals. Religious communities articulate items of their faith into creeds so they can remember what they set out to do in a manner consistent with what they most value. It reminds them of their values. Fortune 500 companies and nonprofit agencies alike adopt mission statements that articulate their values (what drives our company) and vision (where are we going) and of course, their mission (what are doing and what are we about). These statements help the groups stay on a course that is true to their values and purposes. Mission statements work because human beings can simply become tired, challenged, or threatened to a degree that they forget what on earth they were doing to begin with—and their communities and corporations die for a lack of vision.

I hope that this book will help you to understand some of the social and biological underpinnings of your emotional sensitivity, help you validate your emotional experiences, and help you to become aware of your emotions and their helpful functions and learn how to live with your emotions in such a way that they serve you rather than master you.

An Overview of This Book

To give you an idea of what lies ahead, here is a summary of what I plan to cover. The book is divided into four main parts:

Part I: The Nature of Emotion. Here we'll discuss emotions as a "full-system" response, and the purpose they serve in our lives. We'll distinguish between primary and secondary emotions, and we'll try to answer the question: Why do my emotions hurt so much?

Part II: Naming and Describing Your Emotions. This section begins with a series of explanations and exercises about mindfulness, which is a key concept and practice in gaining control over emotions. I'll also talk about emotional triggers, the urges that emotions generate, and the emotional fallout that results from them.

Part III: Reducing Blocks to Emotion Regulation. With a better understanding of how emotions work and what they do in our lives, we can start learning ways to avoid having them dominate us. For starters, we can challenge the self-talk that leads to emotional spirals. We can make changes in our lifestyles that make us physically and emotionally healthier. With the right techniques, we can even confront strong emotions and defuse or redirect them.

Part IV: Leading an Emotionally Skillful Life. This is the payoff, where we turn understanding and technique into skills that we can apply in our daily life. I'll talk about skills in dealing with everyday relationships—including how to deal with difficult people—and our intimate relationships. And finally I'll talk about learning to tolerate and overcome distress, in order to lead a happier, more balanced life.

—Scott Spradlin

PART I

The Nature of Emotion

CHAPTER 1

Emotions: The Full-System Response

What are emotions? Are they thoughts? Are they feelings? Are they the pounding in your chest when you fall in love? Emotions are a full-system response comprising all of these factors and experiences, and they include bodily sensations, the brain, and your thoughts. The word *emotion* itself comes from the Latin *exmovere*, and means to move out, agitate, or excite. This is where our English word "motion" comes from, and of course you can see the connection with the word "emotion." When emotions get stirred up, they bring about movement or action. Emotions are often thought of as strictly feeling or sentiment, but as you will come to see, they're much more encompassing.

Have you ever noticed that when you're emotional you have certain thoughts associated with each emotion? If you're angry, for example, you might think that you hate someone, or that you hate a situation. You might have thoughts such as, "This is so unfair," "I'm in danger," "They have it in for me." In a later chapter we will look at how thoughts—including interpretations, judgments, and beliefs—have the power to influence the emotions that you feel and the intensity of those emotions.

In addition to thoughts, you experience physical urges or agitation. You might want to hit something, buy something, run away, or kiss someone. That's because there's a physiological component to emotion. Here are two other examples of this physiological component. Crying is a physiological activity associated mostly with sadness and grief, but also with happiness, as in "tears of joy." And in the case of anxiety you may notice that you have butterflies in your stomach, especially when you have to speak in front of a crowd, take an exam, deal with your boss, or ask someone out on a date.

When your emotions light up, so does your whole body. A *biological complex* has been activated. You may take off running when you're scared, hug someone when you're happy, get aroused when you feel love, and so on. The biological complex refers to the fact that when you experience emotions they come alive in the completeness of a triggering event, neurochemical activity in the brain, physiological action of the nervous system, respiratory and circulatory systems, thoughts, and overt actions.

So emotion is thought and feeling and disposition to act. There is no emotion without thought, and no thought without emotion. And where there is emotion there is a readiness for action. Emotion is a complex and integrated system, a whole, a gestalt. Each part of the whole is mutually interdependent and the parts cooperate with one another synergistically. Thinking per se is part of feeling, and feeling per se is part of thinking. Information processed cognitively affects emotional states, and primary automatic emotional responses affect cognition, or thinking processes. And within this total matrix is the activity of overall brain and body physiological activity. That's why in this workbook the skills you will learn target thinking (cognition), emotion (affect), and other feelings and urges (physiological urges and activity).

Observables and Unobservables

Emotion researcher and theorist Arnold Lazarus (1991) describes two categories related to human emotional experiences, which he calls *observables* and *unobservables*. Observables can be seen by people around you. They are the overt evidence that you are experiencing emotion. Here are Lazarus's four classes of observables:

1. **Actions**

   - Attack

   - Avoidance

   - Facial expressions

   - Posture

2. **Physiological reactions**

   - Autonomic nervous system

   - Neurological reactions and activity

   - General brain activity

   - Hormonal secretions

3. **What people say**

   - Actual content ("I hate you" or "I love you")

   - Tone of voice (soft, tense, sarcastic, raised)

- Telling others what you feel (sad, happy, angry)

4. Environmental events and contexts

- Social context (dinner, medical appointment, formal or informal)

- Cultural (racial, gender, and locale settings)

- Physical events (war, church service, tornado, etc.)

Here are Lazarus' five classes of unobservables:

1. Action tendencies

- Urges and impulses (to run, attack, talk, take drugs, hurt self)

- A sense of readiness (psyched for the big game)

- May or may not be acted on

- May or may not be recognized by you when you experience them

2. Subjective emotional experiences

- What you or I feel that no one else is aware of

3. Person-environment relationships

- Motives and beliefs of an individual person

- Demands of the environment (work, school, religious community, family)

- Environmental supports, resources, and constraints

- How an individual's motives and beliefs interact with the demands of a given environment

4. Coping process

- How you cope with stresses

- What you use to cope with stress

5. Appraisal processes

- Expectancy of self and environment in relation to one another

- Judgments and assessments of well-being

- Interpretations and philosophies about how things are working, and how they should work

The observables are easier to spot because they're overt and obvious to you and others. But if you're a highly reactive person, you may not be aware of these observables and how they affect your relationships to other people at home, in school, or at work. Also, the more subtle observables, such as posture and facial expression, may require more attention than what you say (telling someone, "Drop dead!") or what you do (throw a plate on the floor).

Some observable factors include events in your environment that affect your emotions. We'll consider these factors when we get to the exercises related to reducing your vulnerabilities and building awareness to the relationship of the environment to your emotions.

Lazarus includes things like hormone secretions and brain activity as observable because scientists can observe and measure them with the right instruments. We'll touch on the role they play in the life of your emotions, but this book won't have you monitoring the secretion of endorphins or serotonin or your brain's electrochemical activity.

As for the unobservables, I will suggest some exercises that specifically help build awareness of these, as they're often off our personal radar screen. These include being mindful to your action tendencies or urges, knowing what you have an urge to do, and increasing your power to decide whether or not you will act on the urge. Remember, you have your own internal experience that no one can see, and there are times when it's important to let others know how and what you're feeling. It can be tough to do this. Others may not "get" the effect their actions have on you. But if they continue to affect you in a negative way and you never tell them, hurt can build up and might end in your telling them off and hurting the relationship.

Just as others don't truly know what our motives or beliefs are, we rarely truly know theirs. Also mysterious is the way in which your and others' motives interact with demands of the environment (community standards, religious, moral, economic, etc.) and whether environmental factors serve as to bolster or stress you and others. Finally, there are coping and appraisal processes, and the way we chose to deal with problems and demands and what we expect of ourselves, and others. These also have to do with how we judge and interpret people's actions and situations.

As you can see, emotions are quite complex in many respects. But don't let this complexity overwhelm you. Just take this workbook one chapter at a time. Take time out to do the exercises. Reread a few chapters. Discuss the material with friends, family, clergy, or a therapist.

The Fusion of Emotions and Thoughts

Are emotions and thoughts separate from one another or are they really just the same thing? For the purpose of this workbook, I think it's important to note that there is a strong connection between emotions and thoughts, or what mental health professionals call *cognitions*.

Since we've been talking about emotion as a full-system response, we can say that emotion consists of parts, or is even a part of the whole of a person. You're probably accustomed to speaking of your emotions as being different than your thoughts. But thinking and emotion are more accurately thought of as being *fused*. We talk about them as distinct from one another in order to better understand their roles as respective parts of the whole system. Later in the book, you will learn and practice skills related specifically to your thoughts.

The reason I mention that thought and emotion are really fused is that when you learn some of the skills in this book, it can be hard to tell if your thoughts come before or after emotions. That's not a yes-or-no proposition, because thoughts sometime come before emotions, with emotions, and after emotions. Thoughts do influence your emotions and emotional states influence your thoughts.

"Raging Steve": A Tale of Driving

Here's a scenario that illustrates the interplay between emotion, action, and the environment, and shows how a primary emotion can spark a secondary one. (We'll cover primary and secondary emotions in chapter 3.)

Let's suppose that while driving home from work one afternoon, Steve gets cut off by another driver. At first he feels some anxiety, which triggers an appropriate reaction: to steer clear of the other car. But within a few seconds, Steve starts thinking, "What a jerk! That guy did that on purpose!" and "No one should drive like that!" His anxiety gives way to anger, anger begets aggression, and pretty soon Steve is chasing the other car down the highway at 70 mph. But the other driver gets away. Why? Because a cop has pulled Steve over and is charging him with several violations, including speeding, failing to signal, etc.

In the above story, Steve rightfully experiences fear, but then his thinking gets the better of him once he is locked onto his assumptions that this man was out to get him specifically, and that this kind of driving *should never* happen. His thoughts compounded his emotions, and told him he needed to show that jerk a thing or two about good driving. His anger was reinforced by angry behaviors, like aggressive driving. Not noticing any of this, he mindlessly and impulsively chased after the other driver. You can see that it was Steve's thinking that continued to prompt and maintain, and even intensify, his anger.

Whether Steve is right or wrong for getting angry isn't important. What matters here is that his indignation at the other person's unsafe driving led him to become an unsafe driver himself, and resulted in a speeding ticket. In the end, his thinking led to ineffective behaviors that made the situation worse.

We all have thoughts that fire with emotions. If they come after a primary emotion, they then may produce a more complicated learned secondary emotional response, like being indignant for a slight to save face (especially for narcissistic or macho types). We can't help it. Evaluations about our well-being, whether for survival or social standing, do factor into our emotional responses and affect our connection with other individuals and our communities. There are times when you might react with a judgment or interpretation about a situation that will trigger emotion or intensify emotion that has already been activated.

You could say that Steve's full system was firing on anger and ramping up to rage.

The Tides of Emotion

Emotions don't last forever, although some last longer than others. Also, the intensity of a given emotion varies from person to person, and can vary from one situation to another. It depends on our current level of skillfulness in handling emotion and other factors such as rest, health, task-related stress, and support. Like the tides of the ocean, emotions ebb and flow, they come and go; they're transitory. This is important to remember when you find yourself in an emotional maelstrom. If you forget that your emotions don't last forever, you may be more likely to act impulsively when you're emotional. But if you're able to tell yourself, in the heat of the moment, "This too shall pass," you'll be a step closer to more effective emotion regulation. You can then open up a variety of options for action, and stretch your willingness to practice your new skills.

If you heat up like a microwave oven and cool down like a conventional one, you may notice that it seems like an eternity to cool down, and as you're cooling down, you're still highly vulnerable to the next trigger.

In the example of Steve the aggressive driver, he was highly angry and agitated, so being pulled over for a ticket will trigger other emotions. Since he is still aroused just following his car chase, if he's not careful, this new event could spike his current anger even further. The more intense the emotion, the more dysregulated Steve feels. He could make things worse yet by swearing at the police officer or complaining that they have more important crimes to track down. If Steve is hopped-up on caffeine or hasn't eaten well, his biological vulnerability will be even higher, making his dysregulation more severe. (In chapter 10, you will learn specific skills for decreasing your vulnerabilities to these and other factors.)

Reflecting on the Ebb and Flow

Take some time to reflect on the last time you experienced strong emotion. Was it today? Yesterday? Just a few moments ago? Whenever that was you will notice, if you reflect, that your emotions vary in how strong they feel. One moment you can be furious enough to throw things, and only moments later feel a tad upset.

Anger

Think of a time when you were so angry that you thought you were going to swear or throw something at someone, or hit or punch them. Think about your angriest moment ever, whatever that might be for you.

Situation: _____

_____

Your thoughts about the situation at the time (how did you interpret it?): _____

_____

Intensity of anger (0-100): _____

Describe the outcomes and consequences at that time (were things the same, made worse, or made better?): _____

_____

How long did it take you to cool down?

Seconds (how many?): _____

Minutes (how many?): _____

Hours (how many?): _____

A day or more (how many?): _____

When you cooled down, what was the strength of your emotion (0-100): _____

Sadness

Think of a time when you were so sad that all you wanted to do was cry, withdraw, avoid others, mope, and be absorbed in sad poems, music, or movies. Think about your saddest moment ever, whatever that might be for you.

Situation: _____

_____

Your thoughts about the situation at the time (how did you interpret it?): _____

_____

Intensity of sadness (0-100): _____

Describe the outcomes and consequences at that time (were things the same, made worse, or made better?): _____

_____

How long did it take you to get back to your normal mood?

Seconds (how many?): _____

Minutes (how many?): _____

Hours (how many?): _____

A day or more (how many?): _____

When you cheered up, what was the strength of your sadness? (0-100): _____

Fear

Think of a time when you were so fearful that all you wanted to do was hide, withdraw, avoid others, panic, or freak out. Think about your most fearful moment, whatever that might be for you.

Situation: _____

_____

Your thoughts about the situation at the time (how did you interpret it?): _____

_____

Intensity of fear (0-100): _____

Describe the outcomes and consequences at that time (were things the same, made worse, or made better?): _____

_____

How long did it take you to cool down?

Seconds (how many?): _____

Minutes (how many?): _____

Hours (how many?): _____

A day or more (how many?): _____

When you relaxed, what was the strength of your fear? (0-100): _____

Love

Think of a time when you were so filled with love that all you wanted to do was think about the person you loved, encourage others, tell friends and family good things about themselves and life, or daydream about beautiful things. Think about your most intense experience of love, whatever that might be for you.

Situation: _____

_____

Your thoughts about the situation at the time (how did you interpret it?): _____

_____

Intensity of love (0-100): _____

Describe the outcomes and consequences at that time (were things the same, made worse, or made better?): _____

_____

How long did it take you to get back to your normal mood?

Seconds (how many?): _____

Minutes (how many?): _____

Hours (how many?): _____

A day or more (how many?): _____

When your feeling of love leveled off, what was the strength of love (0-100): _____

Happiness/Joy

Think of a time when you were so happy that all you did was laugh, you cheered up others around you, and you felt strong, confident, and positive. Think about your most happy or joyful moment ever, whatever that might be for you.

Situation: _____

_____

Your thoughts about the situation at the time (how did you interpret it?): _____

_____

Intensity of happiness/joy (0-100): _____

Describe the outcomes and consequences at that time (were things the same, made worse, or made better?): _____

_____

How long did it take you to "come down" or get back to your normal mood?

   Seconds (how many?): _____

   Minutes (how many?): _____

   Hours (how many?): _____

   A day or more (how many?): _____

When you "came down," what was the strength of happiness/joy (0-100): _____

Emotion States, Traits, and Moods

An *emotion state* is that discrete affective moment when you can say, "I feel anger." It is transient, part of the ebb and flow we mentioned above. An *emotion trait* is more enduring and is characteristic of a person. If you tend to respond to situations with frustration and anger, you might say, "I'm an angry person." To quote Lazarus again, "An emotion *trait* refers to a characteristic of a person, and so is not really an emotion, but a *disposition* or tendency to react with one" (1991, 46).

You may have a particular emotion that you experience more often than other emotions. Folks around you may know you as a "sad person," an "angry person," or a "happy person." A "happy person," isn't always and ever a happy person, since they do in fact feel anger, sadness, and anxiety. We all do. A happy person is a person who seems more *generally* happy, and perhaps responds to the world with more positive actions and thoughts about what happens, outcomes, and their ability to deal with challenges. An anxious person is someone who tends to respond to challenges, or even the thought of challenges, with worry. This is the "worrywart," and an anxious person may have predominantly worrisome thoughts and actions. Like happy people, anxious people don't feel only anxiety. They also feel joy, love, and anger. Anxious people can also have dreams and hopeful thoughts.

Finally, there are *moods*. Basically, moods are emotions that stick around for a really long time. And just as a happy person will feel anger or sadness and an anxious person will feel the emotion of happiness, a happy person can have a blue or depressed mood, perhaps due to illness or circumstances. And while some emotions stick around longer than others, they tend not to last forever. Moods that become predominant and stick around too long become *mood disorders,* such as severe and chronic depression, or generalized anxiety disorder.

As you practice the skills in this workbook, you'll find it important to increase your awareness of the range of emotions that you feel. If you're a happy person, it can seem as though you never get angry. If you're a worrywart, in moments of anxiety it can seem as though you never feel happy. Getting stuck on a thought such as "I never feel happy, life always sucks," will perpetuate anxiety or sadness, and will inevitably affect your emotional state.

Here is a list of corresponding states, traits, and moods.

- State: Love
- Trait: Loving or caring
- Mood: Euphoria

- State: Fear
- Trait: Fearful
- Mood: Anxiety

- State: Anger
- Trait: Angry
- Mood: Irritable

The Joy Will End, but So Will the Pain

As you work through the exercises in this book, I hope you will remember that emotion comes and goes. That's important to know because it can help keep you from becoming overly expectant to feel good all of the time. Such expectations inevitably lead to disappointment, and you may even consider yourself a failure at having the good life, as it were, and perhaps induce unnecessary emotional suffering. Conversely, when you're distraught or dysregulated, and already suffering, you can remind yourself that your pain will stop eventually. Just like the positive and pleasant emotions, the painful ones will also end. Neither positive nor negative emotions last forever.

If you're a person who wishes they could feel good all of the time, you're not alone. But that's not the order of things, that's not reality. Accept those negative times along with the good and positive, because you can't have one without the other. Just as there is night and day, there is sadness and happiness. The biological components of emotion and the parts of your brain that let you feel emotion and receive all of the important information that comes through that system require that you feel both pain and joy.

CHAPTER 2

What Are Emotions For?

If you're reading this book to learn how to live effectively with your emotions, you probably sometimes wonder why we're emotional at all. What good are emotions, anyway? Researchers don't all agree on exactly what emotions seem to be for and what good they can do us, but they share a general area of agreement. This summary by emotion experts Greenberg and Paivio (1997) captures some of these generally agreed upon main functions. Emotions:

- Prompt and organize us for action

- Give us important information about what's going on in a given situation

- Are for motivating

- Are for communicating to others

- Are fundamentally adaptive

The Function of Emotions

Let's consider the above summary in a bit more detail.

Emotions prompt and organize us for action

When a particular emotion is triggered, your whole body goes on a sort of alert to be ready for action related to that emotion. Anger can organize you mentally and physiologically to become aggressive. Fear will get you ready to flee, if necessary; your mind begins thinking fear-related thoughts, and your body is primed to run for safety. Your entire biological makeup is primed to take action consistent with whatever emotion has been triggered.

Emotions give us important information about what's going on in a given situation

Emotions are like a motion-detection or warning system telling us that something is happening in our environment that we should know about. This warning system can alert us to physical danger, or give us information about how a social interaction is going. It's important to be aware of your emotions so that you can hear what they are telling you, because they can alert you to danger or to love. Paying attention to what information your emotions give you can make a difference in your safety or assist you with improving relationships. In both cases, emotions may tell you that you need to change a behavior to become more effective at meeting your needs or at forging quality relationships.

Emotions are for motivating

To return to the very word itself, "motion," emotions get you going to do things. These may be work, relationships, or seeking food or well-being. Strong emotions can serve you in overcoming obstacles between you and something you want. Jealousy may motivate you to protect a relationship by being more attentive to your partner. Anger may lead you to stand up for your rights when you're being mistreated. People who suffer from depression or schizophrenia, or who have long histories of drug or alcohol dependency, often experience *avolition*, which is the loss of any sense of emotion as demonstrated by a lack of goal-directed behaviors. These people often lose jobs and relationships, and they can become accident victims because they don't register the emotional feedback they need to maintain their safety.

Emotions are for communicating to others

Emotions help us communicate of ourselves to other people. They may prime us to provide direct verbal content to another person, but emotions do more than get us to say words. We also use facial expressions, gestures, and tone of voice to communicate. If we aren't aware of how we appear to others when we are trying to communicate to them, we may not communicate effectively what we want to get across.

For example, suppose your male partner has hurt your feelings with a sarcastic comment about your appearance. Your emotion might be sadness. If you attack your partner, however, he may not realize or understand that his comments hurt your feelings; he might think you're just being aggressive. Whereas if you're mindful of your sadness, and you let yourself feel and show that sadness to your partner, you'll be better able to show him that you're sad, and not angry.

Sometimes you might be feeling an emotion strongly, but you need to engage in an activity where expressing that emotion isn't appropriate, such as taking a job interview. That's obviously the wrong time to appear sad or angry; you want to appear confident and competent. To do that, you need to know what you feel, how you're likely to act or appear when having that emotion, and then decide to make sure that your emotions communicate what they need to at that time.

Emotions are fundamentally adaptive

All that has been said above is summed up in this statement: Emotions are inherently, essentially, fundamentally adaptive. That is, your emotions are helpers. Sometimes I liken emotions to shepherds that try to guide us to safety and well-being. Even painful emotions such as fear can guide us away from danger. Love can guide us to build and enhance relationships. Interest can help us to expand our learning and self-mastery through learning.

If you have written off your emotions because you sometimes find yourself being too emotional, it's time to change your mind. It's time to learn the natural functions and advantages of emotions while also realizing that you will always face making mistakes and feeling strongly. If you get off track, the skills you can learn in this book will help you to get back on track again.

The Physiology of Emotion

The following will better illustrate how emotions are a full-system, total-person response. In his 1995 book, *Emotional Intelligence*, Daniel Goleman summarizes the connection between the physiological components of emotions and their apparent functions.

Anger

Blood flows to the hands, making it easier to grasp a weapon or strike at a foe. The heart rate increases, and a rush of hormones such as adrenaline generates a pulse of energy for vigorous action.

Fear

Blood goes to the large skeletal muscles, such as the legs, making it easier to flee. It also makes the face blanch as blood is shunted away from it, creating the feeling of "having your blood run cold." At the same time, the body freezes, if only for a moment, perhaps allowing time to gauge whether hiding might be a better reaction than fleeing. Circuits in the brain's emotional centers trigger a flood of hormones that put the body on general alert, making it edgy and ready for action. Attention focuses on the threat at hand, the better to evaluate what response to make.

Happiness

Happiness increases activity in a brain center that inhibits negative feelings and fosters an increase in available energy, and causes a quieting of those areas that generate worrisome thought. But there is no particular shift in physiology save a quiescence that helps the body recover more quickly from the biological arousal of upsetting emotions. This configuration offers the body general rest, as well as readiness and enthusiasm for whatever task is at hand and for striving toward a variety of goals.

Love

Tender feelings and sexual satisfaction entail parasympathetic arousal, the physiological opposite of the fight-or-flight mobilization shared by fear and anger. The parasympathetic pattern, dubbed *relaxation response*, is a body-wide set of reactions that generates a general state of calm and contentment, facilitating cooperation.

Surprise

Lifting your eyebrows enlarges your visual field and lets more light strike the retina. This yields more information about the unexpected event, making it easier to figure out exactly what is going on and concoct the best plan for action.

Disgust

The expression for disgust is universal, say anthropological studies on human facial and emotional expressions. Disgust sends a message: something is offensive in taste or smell, or metaphorically so. The facial expression of disgust—the upper lip curled to the side as the nose wrinkles slightly—suggests an attempt to close the nostrils against noxious odors or to spit out a poisonous food.

Sadness

Sadness helps us adjust to a significant loss, such as the death of someone close or a major disappointment. Sadness brings a drop in energy and enthusiasm for life's activities, particularly diversions and pleasures. As it deepens and approaches depression, it slows the body's metabolism. This introspective withdrawal creates an opportunity to mourn a loss or frustrated hope, grasp its consequences for one's life, and, as energy returns, plan new beginnings. This loss of energy may well have kept saddened—and vulnerable—people of tribal cultures and primitive times close to home, where they were safe.

Emotions as Helpers

Emotions get us ready to act. They get our engines of action primed and running. They do this by acting as alarms, telling us something is going on, sometimes quickly enough that we don't have to think things through all of the time. We can also say that while thoughts affect emotions, they aren't necessarily mediating every emotional response, at least at a conscious level. Emotions can get us going efficiently, and this works in some circumstances but not in others.

In this chapter, we discussed the important things emotions do for us: preparing for action, gathering information, and communicating with other people. In the next chapter you'll learn about the difference between primary and secondary emotions, and you'll have an opportunity to practice your awareness of the function of your emotions.

CHAPTER 3

Primary and Secondary Emotions

When emotions do what they're supposed to do, they're referred to as *primary emotions*. They're uncomplicated, unlearned responses that are fundamental to human functioning. Primary emotions aren't complicated mixtures of various emotions, and they don't necessarily require that we "think things through." They are part of the hard-wired biological component of emotions, and most researchers agree that they are related to survival.

When you hear a loud noise and you jump or duck to the ground, your body reacted with a primary fear reaction in order to protect you from a perceived threat. Someone you like asks you out to lunch, and you feel elated and joyful. Your beloved pet dies, and you cry because you have lost something dear to you. None of these are dysfunctional, and nearly all people feel emotions and feel a range of intensity of these emotions.

Emotion researchers aren't unanimous on how many primary emotions exist or exactly how to define them, but most recognize nine primary emotions:

- Joy
- Love
- Interest
- Sorrow

- Surprise

- Fear

- Disgust

- Guilt

- Anger

The "Foaming Doggie" Story

As an example of primary emotions I often tell my clients in DBT skills groups a fictitious story about the "foaming doggie." Here's the scenario: I'm crossing the street to go to the local convenience store to buy myself a soda. As I cross the street I notice a dog trotting straight for me. It's a rottweiler, it has massive amounts of foam around the mouth, and it's growling in a very unfriendly way. I notice that my heart rate speeds up, I feel adrenaline surge through my body, and before I can think about it, I'm running for the door of the convenience store. Once inside, I'm safe. While the store clerk telephones the animal control service, my heart rate and adrenaline slowly return to normal.

What happened? My emotions did me a very big favor. My brain recognized this animal as a dog, and also registered the foam as a potential symptom of rabies. On hearing the growling, which is usually a sign of hostility, my body took over before I had time to ask myself, "Gee, I wonder if puppy is friendly?" This fear response is an example of unlearned basic and primary emotional response.

Exploring Primary Emotions

Look over the following list and check the items you identify with. These are intended to help you think of and become aware of times when emotions have been helpful to you. That is, how have these emotions been functional or adaptive? After each item that you check, take a moment to write a bit about the situation in which you found the emotion to be helpful. Describe what you experienced and what you did.

Joy and happiness have helped me to ...

- Initiate relationships

    Describe: _____

    _____

- Get energized for daily tasks

    Describe: _____

    _____

- Cope with sickness

  Describe: _____

  _____

- Find hope in difficult situations

  Describe: _____

  _____

- Donate my time and/or money to charity

  Describe: _____

  _____

- Encourage other people around me

  Describe: _____

  _____

- Express thanks to others who have helped me

  Describe: _____

  _____

- Other

  Describe: _____

  _____

Love has helped me to ...

- Enhance relationships

  Describe: _____

  _____

- Forgive someone who has wronged me

  Describe: _____

  _____

- Tell others that I love them with a letter, card, e-mail, or phone call

  Describe: _____

  _____

- Buy gifts for the people I love

  Describe: _____

  _____

- Other

  Describe: _____

  _____

Fear has helped me to ...

- Avoid dangerous animals

  Describe: _____

  _____

- Keep from falling off a roof or cliff

  Describe: _____

  _____

- Prevent my being victimized

  Describe: _____

  _____

- Swerve out of the way of oncoming traffic while driving

  Describe: _____

  _____

- Other:

  Describe: _____

  _____

Guilt has helped me to ...

- Know when I have offended someone I care about

  Describe: _____

  _____

- Know when I'm acting against my own values

  Describe: _____

  _____

- Make amends and relationship repair to someone I have hurt

  Describe: _____

  _____

- Change and correct self-defeating behaviors

  Describe: _____

  _____

- Other:

  Describe: _____

  _____

Secondary Emotions

Secondary emotions are called secondary because they aren't necessarily related to an adaptive response in a given situation. Also, they come "second," behind primary emotional responses. Secondary emotions are complicated, non-adaptive patterns of emotions *about* emotions. They come to us through a filter of thought processes that go by many names: automatic thoughts, judgments, assumptions, or irrational beliefs. These complex emotions are learned responses that often come from role models, usually in our family of origin.

Here are some examples of secondary emotions:

- Feeling angry about feeling angry

- Feeling angry about feeling sad

- Feeling shame for feeling fear

- Feeling anxious about feeling fear

- Feeling sad about feeling sad

How do you learn these secondary emotional responses? You likely first learned them in your childhood from the adults in your immediate family. Those who are closest to you in the very early and informative years of your life exude a great influence, even when they don't intend to. If you witnessed your parents becoming angry about being angry or agitated over their own emotion, that will influence how you come to understand—or think you understand—how emotions work.

How your family reacted to your communication of your own internal emotional experiences can also affect how you come to have these secondary emotional responses. For example, a little boy who scrapes his knee doesn't know what the pain means to the degree that a grown person might. His crying may be activated by fear of being seriously injured. If he's then told, "Boys don't cry," he receives a cultural message about what is expected of him as a male. This message can become over-generalized. Later in life, when the boy becomes a man, he may feel sadness in situations where he is faced with loss or pain. But because of his cultural training, the man tries to cut off his emotions, or may tell himself that he's just being too sensitive. He doesn't validate his primary emotion, and then begins to feel shame about having been sensitive. The shame in this case becomes the secondary emotion, and isn't helpful in adapting to his current situation. For him, the message, "Boys don't cry," becomes a lifelong mandate.

Revisiting the "Foaming Doggie"

For another example of secondary emotion, let's revisit the foaming doggie story. You remember that I felt fear, and that primary fear activated my whole emotional system to get me to safety, which it did, so it was effective.

This time, let's say that once I was inside the store, I encounter a group of other men, a bunch of tough construction workers. They start to laugh at me, and I can hear them saying to themselves, "What a wimp!" "Man, that guy's a chicken, running from that dog," and so on. Worse, the clerk now joins the laughter.

I might feel embarrassed about having been fearful, even though my fear wasn't about manliness. It was about avoiding getting chomped and having to get rabies shots. But if I interpret myself as weak, chicken, or unmanly I might feel intensely ashamed of myself. Or I might become enraged at these guys for making fun of me. Maybe I'd want to hit them but dare not, because I'm outnumbered. Also, it would be unprofessional, and I care about having a good standing in the community. I could carry that with me all day, just feeling miserable. That's an example of secondary emotion, and it's a typically complicated, unhelpful mess.

Instances of Secondary Emotions

People often try to deal with their secondary emotions through impulsive behaviors. They may hit or yell at people they're angry with, or attempt to soothe themselves by overeating, binging, overusing alcohol, misusing prescription meds, cutting themselves, and so on. These impulsive behaviors can be successful in momentarily quelling the emotion, but they can become long-standing behavioral responses to emotional crises, and ultimately unhelpful.

Here are some examples of secondary emotions. Read over the list, check all that you identify with, and then write a brief description about what you felt and what you did:

Feeling angry about being angry

Describe: _____

_____

Feeling angry about crying

Describe: _____

_____

Feeling shame for having been embarrassed

Describe: _____

_____

Feeling ashamed for having been angry

Describe: _____

_____

Feeling self-disgust for being sad or angry

Describe: _____

_____

Feeling anxious about feeling anxious

Describe: _____

_____

Feeling guilty for having felt happy or joyful

Describe: _____

_____

Feeling worry about joy or happiness ending

Describe: _____

_____

Insights into Secondary Emotions

The biggest problem with secondary emotions is that they usually don't help you adapt to your circumstances, either biologically or socially. Very often, they're generated and intensified by judgments we have about how we are *supposed* to feel in a given situation, instead of how we *actually* feel. It's my hope that this book will help you to be more spontaneous and to become increasingly free from secondary emotional responses, increasingly balanced, and more skillful and more effective in your relationships and life's pursuits.

In the next chapter, we'll explore some factors that can increase the strength of our emotions. Some are purely biological, and beyond our immediate control. But many are within our reach, and can be examined and changed. Some, like eating or sleeping poorly, make us physically vulnerable to strong emotion. Others, such as negative judgments and self-talk, are internal. Learning about both kinds is the first step in changing them.

PART II

Naming and Describing
Your Emotins

CHAPTER 4

Why Do My Emotions Hurt So Much?

We've established that emotions have functions and uses, but so what? You may be having such a rough time with your emotions that you think no survival function is worth the intensity and chaos that you feel. But let me tell you, it's not just the sensitive people who feel painful emotions like sadness and fear—we all do. However, we experience our emotions with varying degrees of intensity, and there are factors that may be increasing the intensity with which you feel them. The factors to consider include:

- Biology

- Vulnerability factors

- Judgments and secondary emotional responses

- Modeling and learning factors, and other environmental factors

Biology and Emotion

As we've said, your emotions are in part biologically hard-wired. You can't experience your emotions without your brain getting involved. And when your brain is involved there are numerous hormones and neurotransmitters that get involved, too. The way that each of us experiences our emotions is affected by the shape of particular parts of the brain, certain levels of one hormone or another, and all of these are affected by our diet, sleep habits, and so forth. Later we will look at changes that you can make in your lifestyle to increase your emotional resilience. For now, here are some of the chemicals in our bodies that are involved in emotion:

Cortisol. This hormone is important in helping the body metabolize proteins and carbohydrates and is related to coping with stress and fatigue. Recent studies suggest that individuals with lower baselines of production of cortisol are predisposed to post-traumatic stress disorder (PTSD), problems with attention, and impulsivity. In some individuals, unusually high levels of cortisol are released into the brain at the time of a traumatic event. With prolonged stress or trauma, cortisol levels appear to drop, but traumatized individuals demonstrate an especially heightened sensitivity to the amounts that are produced in their bodies, and this may have some relationship to the experiences of flashbacks.

Serotonin. This hormone has a wide array of functions, including emotion control, perceptions, and mood modulation in response to stressful events. For those who suffer from depression it is thought that their brains don't produce enough serotonin or use it effectively. These deficiencies contribute greatly to depressed mood. Carbohydrates and exercise help increase serotonin levels. The anti-depressants known as serotonin reuptake inhibitors (SSRIs) recycle serotonin in the brain and make more of it available.

Endorphins. Related to feeling good and pleasure, endorphins are produced in response to touch and exercise. If you've ever heard of "runner's high," this is a short-hand way to talk about the experience of increased endorphins. Endorphins and human touch are so important to us that newborns who aren't regularly held and touched are more likely to die prematurely than those who are.

Vulnerabilities

Vulnerability factors increase your reactivity and susceptibility to being too emotional and impulsive, or to emotional suffering. Even people who are generally unflappable are vulnerable to being overly emotional when they are fatigued, becoming more easily angered and irritable. The antidote? Well, in this case, sleep. If you've been amping up on coffee all day you will be more likely to fidget or become anxious.

Look at the following list of vulnerability factors and check all that apply to you, and then add others you may be aware of but that aren't on the list. By building awareness of your vulnerabilities, you learn how you can then reduce them. Vulnerability factors include:

- Too much or too little sleep
- Too much junk food
- Dehydration
- Too much caffeine

- Hunger and poor nutrition

- Overeating and under eating

- Injuries or wounds

- Physical or medical illness

- Financial problems

- Underemployment or unemployment

- Overworking

- Eating too much sugar

- Eating too much fat

- Recent losses or accidents

- Recent natural disasters

- Recent relationship difficulties

- Being a victim of crime (assault, rape, theft, etc.)

- Lack of exercise

- Fatigue

- Dwelling on recent personal failure

Other: _____

Judgments, Self-Talk, and Interpretations

Vulnerabilities also affect our thought processes for the worse. The more run down or reactive you feel, the more likely you are to think less of yourself. If you're a man, and you think of yourself as a sissy for experiencing fear or for experiencing sadness, you may feel worse. Your emotion won't simply be fear or sadness, but fear about fear, sadness about sadness, and maybe shame about both of these. Perhaps you judge yourself as being weak-willed, crazy, or having "lost it." Your automatic thoughts and judgments will affect the way you experience your emotions. And these judgments often lead to secondary emotions, which don't help us with survival, social connection, or general well-being.

If you thought about it, you would likely discover that your judgments about your emotions are learned, coming from your environment through modeling how to express, control, or think about feelings. This can happen either implicitly or explicitly. What judgments do you have about your emotions, and where did they come from?

Take a moment to check the items on the following list that you identify with. In the blank next to each, write the source of this belief. Then write out the pros and cons of holding that belief. Pros for holding any belief might include that it's just easier to hold your beliefs as they are since there's no extra work to be done. A con might be that you continue in your same old patterns, doing ineffective business as usual.

Judgments and Automatic Thoughts

- **Emotions are bad and dumb.**

    Rate strength of belief: *1 2 3 4 5*

    Where did this belief come from? _____

    Pros and cons of holding this belief:

    Pros: _____   *Cons:* _____

    _____   _____

    _____   _____

- **My emotions aren't important.**

    Rate strength of belief: *1 2 3 4 5*

    Where did this belief come from? _____

    Pros and cons of holding this belief:

    Pros: _____   *Cons:* _____

    _____   _____

    _____   _____

- **Others don't care about my feelings, so I shouldn't care either.**

    Rate strength of belief: *1 2 3 4 5*

    Where did this belief come from? _____

    Pros and cons of holding this belief:

    Pros: _____   *Cons:* _____

    _____   _____

    _____   _____

- **Expressing my feelings is a sign of weakness.**

    Rate strength of belief: *1 2 3 4 5*

    Where did this belief come from? _____

    Pros and cons of holding this belief:

    Pros: _____   *Cons:* _____

    _____   _____

- **Being emotional is the same as being out of control.**

   Rate strength of belief: *1 2 3 4 5*

   Where did this belief come from? _____

   Pros and cons of holding this belief:

   Pros: _____ *Cons:* _____

   _____ _____

   _____ _____

- **Anger isn't for women.**

   Rate strength of belief: *1 2 3 4 5*

   Where did this belief come from? _____

   Pros and cons of holding this belief:

   Pros: _____ *Cons:* _____

   _____ _____

   _____ _____

- **Fear isn't for men.**

   Rate strength of belief: *1 2 3 4 5*

   Where did this belief come from? _____

   Pros and cons of holding this belief:

   Pros: _____ *Cons:* _____

   _____ _____

   _____ _____

- **I should never feel afraid.**

   Rate strength of belief: *1 2 3 4 5*

   Where did this belief come from? _____

   Pros and cons of holding this belief:

   Pros: _____ *Cons:* _____

   _____ _____

   _____ _____

- **Being emotional is a sign that I'm weak.**

  Rate strength of belief: *1 2 3 4 5*

  Where did this belief come from? _____

  Pros and cons of holding this belief:

  Pros: _____   *Cons:* _____

  _____   _____

  _____   _____

- **Emotions always get in the way.**

  Rate strength of belief: *1 2 3 4 5*

  Where did this belief come from? _____

  Pros and cons of holding this belief:

  Pros: _____   *Cons:* _____

  _____   _____

  _____   _____

- **Emotions are for the hysterical.**

  Rate strength of belief: *1 2 3 4 5*

  Where did this belief come from? _____

  Pros and cons of holding this belief:

  Pros: _____   *Cons:* _____

  _____   _____

  _____   _____

- **I wish I never felt anything.**

  Rate strength of belief: *1 2 3 4 5*

  Where did this belief come from? _____

  Pros and cons of holding this belief:

  Pros: _____   *Cons:* _____

  _____   _____

  _____   _____

- **There is never a right time for strong emotions.**

  Rate strength of belief: *1 2 3 4 5*

  Where did this belief come from? _____

  Pros and cons of holding this belief:

  Pros: _____ *Cons:* _____

      _____   _____

      _____   _____

- **I'm afraid of my emotions.**

  Rate strength of belief: *1 2 3 4 5*

  Where did this belief come from? _____

  Pros and cons of holding this belief:

  Pros: _____ *Cons:* _____

      _____   _____

      _____   _____

Any others? Use the space below to write down any thoughts or beliefs about emotion you may hold that aren't reflected in the above choices. Make sure to include the sources for each of the additional beliefs as you think of them, and include the pros and cons of holding the beliefs.

_____

_____

_____

_____

Ranking Your Thoughts

Out of the above automatic thoughts and beliefs you have about your emotions, take the top five and list them in the following numbered blanks (1-5) and write in the degree to which you believe each one (1-5). Once you finish this exercise, take a moment to look at chapter 9, "Challenging Your Self-Talk."

Top Five Beliefs

1. _____

2. _____

3. _____

4. _____

5. _____

Modeling, Invalidation, and Other Environmental Sources

Your secondary emotional responses sometimes get in the way of your primary responses. You can become so dysregulated that you forget what you felt about something in the first place. Instead of simply letting your emotions do their job when appropriate, or simply validating them, you reject your emotions as invalid, inaccurate, and ultimately unimportant. You treat your sadness as though it's a weakness rather than an informant alerting you to what's important to you in your life.

If you think about your family when you were growing up, I'm sure you can remember instances of how your parents responded to your emotional communications. I don't necessarily mean an explicit message like, "Suck it up." The message is often more subtle. For example, were you ever spoken to angrily or even threateningly when you were crying? That would be a message that your parents disapproved of your display of emotion. In my sadly realistic example, the angry parent doesn't say, "Gee, Timmy, mommy doesn't like it when you cry. In fact, I feel angry and would like you to stop crying now." More likely, she said, "I'll give you something to cry about!"

How did your parents display their own emotions? Did they appear to be terribly reserved and repressed, or did they fly off the handle at every provocation? Were they consistent or inconsistent? What is modeled to us as children has a profound effect throughout our entire lives about how to live with our emotions. We seem to record the patterns of our parents to some degree or another.

You may have been the sensitive, reactive, and emotional one in your family. That's neither good nor bad, that's just the way it is. But if you displayed intense responses in a family with a very low tolerance for emotional displays, you may have faced repeated invalidating responses to your outbursts. Invalidation would be responses from your family and environment that tell you that your private emotional experiences, and certainly your public communications of emotion aren't legitimate in their own right or worth paying attention to and are better stuffed or kept silent.

The problem here is that while you might shut up for a while, temporarily making things easier for others, it doesn't teach you how to effectively solve problems, nor does it teach you how to label your emotions. Sometimes, this oversimplification of your problems and emotional experiences is the path to behaviors that are so extreme they force the people around you to notice your pain and take you seriously. So if you're also struggling with particular behaviors such as self-harm, suicide threats, rages, or other ways of "acting out," there is a function within the apparent dysfunction of such behaviors.

If you have engaged in any of these behaviors, you may notice how the environment will take notice, because these "in-your-face" behaviors can't be ignored. When the world comes to your aid, and validates you in these extreme moments, the problem behaviors are strengthened—reinforced—and likely to happen again. And why wouldn't they? The behaviors got you validation, which is something we all need and want.

Did You Ever Experience Invalidation?

Take a look at the following statements and check all that you identify with having had the statement communicated about you or to you. You'll notice that some statements are dismissive of needs, while others are direct put-downs. The idea of this exercise is to help you build your awareness of your experiences. Mark statements only if you can recall receiving the statement as a consistent message for a good deal of your upbringing. If you check three or more, there's a good chance you were raised in an invalidating environment.

- You're just a big baby

- Why can't you be more like your brother/sister/friend, etc.?

- If you don't stop crying I'll give you something to cry about

- Boys don't cry

- Crying is for sissies

- Your problem is that you're lazy

- You're just good-for-nothing

- Don't make such a fuss

- You're so sensitive

- You're never happy with anything

- Shut up!

- You're so stupid

- You're such an embarrassment

- Stop whining, it's annoying

- Good kids don't complain

- Why are you always complaining?

- You eat like a pig

- Are you talking back to me?

Other: _____

_____

_____

Think of familiar memories of situations that occurred frequently in your childhood in which you can recall experiencing invalidation, such as being sad and crying but being told, "I'll give you something to cry about," or "Boys don't cry," or being told to shut up. Or describe how your attempts to express your internal feelings and experiences were met with indifference. Using a situation that occurred often will make it easier for you to identify your experiences of being invalidated. Don't make things up, or exaggerate your memories. Just do your best to remember what you tried to express, to whom, how they responded, and how you felt and how you believe it affects you to this date. If you live or work with someone currently whom you believe is invalidating, you may use situations from your interactions with them.

Describing Invalidation

Invalidating situation #1

Describe the situation including who and where: _____

_____

_____

What were you trying to express? _____

_____

_____

How were you invalidated? Were you called names, ignored, or did you have your needs minimized? _____

_____

_____

What emotions and thoughts did you have when you were invalidated? _____

_____

_____

What did you do in response to the invalidation? Was this effective or ineffective?

_____

_____

_____

What did you feel and think after trying to cope with invalidation? _____

_____

_____

How do you think this experience affects you in your life today? _____

_____

_____

Invalidating situation #2

Describe the situation including who and where: _____

_____

_____

What were you trying to express? _____

_____

_____

How were you invalidated? Were you called names, ignored, or did you have your needs minimized? _____

_____

_____

What emotions and thoughts did you have when you were invalidated? _____

_____

_____

What did you do in response to the invalidation? Was this effective or ineffective?

_____

_____

_____

What did you feel and think after trying to cope with invalidation? _____

_____

_____

How do you think this experience affects you in your life today? _____

_____

_____

Invalidating situation #3

Describe the situation including who and where: _____

_____

_____

What were you trying to express? _____

_____

_____

How were you invalidated? Were you called names, ignored, or did you have your needs minimized? _____

_____

_____

What emotions and thoughts did you have when you were invalidated? _____

_____

_____

What did you do in response to the invalidation? Was this effective or ineffective?

_____

_____

_____

What did you feel and think after trying to cope with invalidation? _____

_____

_____

How do you think this experience affects you in your life today? _____

_____

_____

Reflecting on Invalidation

One problem with having experienced invalidation during your formative years is that you probably weren't taught effective skills for identifying your emotions, self-soothing, or problem solving. Invalidation treats your problems as unimportant, and an invalidating environment may attribute your lack of problem-solving skills to some undesirable trait such as laziness or stupidity. This can be very frustrating.

Another problem is that you can take these messages of invalidation with you into your adult life, and begin to invalidate yourself. You may develop patterns of second-guessing yourself, not taking your own problems seriously, or becoming overly dependent on your environment to decide what you should be doing, thinking, feeling, or even wanting.

Take a moment to reflect on whether and how you may have internalized invalidation. You may notice that if you have internalized invalidation, that it may have come over the course of your life, beginning in your childhood. You may notice that these past experiences or the internalized invalidation make it difficult for you to handle certain kinds of people or situations, perhaps because they remind you of those past circumstances. Later, in chapter 9, we will explore ways to challenge this internalized invalidation.

Awareness of Self-Invalidation

What invalidating messages from your upbringing do you tell yourself these days?

_____

_____

_____

What situations are most likely to trigger self-invalidation? _____

_____

_____

Describe if/how you try to ignore your feelings, thoughts, wants: _____

_____

_____

Describe if/how you oversimplify the problems and challenges you face in your life:

_____

_____

_____

Describe how you think your self-invalidation affects how you feel and think about yourself: _____

_____

_____

Your Emotional Role Models

As a child, you probably learned patterns from others by watching how they dealt with their emotions, expressing them or denying them, or being overly reactive themselves.

Make a list of the major emotional role models in your family, or from your childhood and adolescence. List your parents, guardians, uncles, aunts, siblings, grandparents, caregivers, teachers, clergy, etc.

My emotional role models were:

1. _____

2. _____

3. _____

4. _____

5. _____

Other: _____

_____

_____

Next, rewrite your list below, using up to five people that you think were most influential. If your list of the most influential is shorter, then work with that. Then, in the space provided below each person's name, list their dominant emotional style (their general emotional trait), then write a brief summary about how you remember these persons.

Think through if you remember them as angry, peaceful, balance, imbalanced, depressed, anxious, etc. Finally, summarize what you think you may have learned from each of these individuals. For example, did you learn to ignore your emotions? Did you learn emotional balance? Did you learn to take your emotions seriously? Did you learn to be out of control or chronically angry, or how to judge others for displaying their emotions, and so on.

You may include in this summary your opinion about whether these models and their lessons have been effective or detrimental to you.

Emotional role model #1: _____

Emotional style: _____

What I learned from this person: _____

_____

_____

_____

_____

Emotional role model #2: _____

Emotional style: _____

What I learned from this person: _____

_____

_____

_____

_____

Emotional role model #3: _____

Emotional style: _____

What I learned from this person: _____

_____

_____

_____

_____

Emotional role model #4: _____

Emotional style: _____

What I learned from this person: _____

_____

_____

_____

_____

Emotional role model #5: _____

Emotional style: _____

What I learned from this person: _____

_____

_____

_____

_____

Sources of Emotional Pain

I hope the above exercises give you a clearer picture of why emotions can be so intensely painful.

To summarize, there is the biological gear that you come with hard-wired into you. Whether there were in vivo traumas, head injuries, chronic stressors, or nutritional influences, a great deal of what you experience is simply your body and brain doing what they do naturally. They have nothing to do with your good or bad attitude. Next, depending on your general state of rest, fluid intake, nutrition, medication, unexpected emergencies, illness, etc., your general baseline mood will be affected. These factors will influence your emotional arousal and cooling down, and your own appraisal of how you think you may or may not be able to cope. Another factor is what you say to yourself when you become emotionally aroused, since your thoughts can affect your control of emotion. Finally, what you learned about your emotions from your emotional role models provide a sort of template for how to relate to your emotions.

In the next chapter, we'll move from general awareness of our emotions to the special kind of self-knowing called mindfulness.

CHAPTER 5

Mindfulness to Emotion

What is this thing called mindfulness? It is a practice of being awake, of participating in your life, of learning to inhabit your life. It is also a practice of becoming more intentional with your actions. This combines two vital aspects of mindfulness: attention and intention. With respect to emotion it's about becoming more mindful to—aware of—the emotions you experience, as you're experiencing them.

Mindfulness is something of a paradox. It is both easy and difficult. It is easy thanks the fact that you have all the necessary equipment with you wherever you go and nearly every situation in life presents you with an opportunity to practice. It's hard because so much of our world and our habits militate against it.

Believe it or not, this skill of mindfulness is a big help for sensitive people. Much of the psychological data and literature on emotional intelligence strongly suggests a relationship connecting awareness to emotion regulation. In DBT, the concept of mindfulness is borrowed from traditional meditation practices, but it isn't exactly meditation. You don't have to sit in the lotus position, or close your eyes, or fast, or chant. There may be a time and place for those more formal practices, and I suggest you consider them. But right now, you can practice mindfulness skills in your everyday life that can be very helpful in regulating emotion.

The Nature of Mindfulness

Let me start by making some important clarifications about the practice of mindfulness, as I understand it.

Mindfulness is:

- Becoming more *aware*

- Becoming more *intentional*

- Becoming more *participatory* in your own life and experiences

- Becoming more *present* and *alive* in each moment you live

Mindfulness is *not* (necessarily):

- Relaxation (although you might experience this)

- Navel-gazing or escape from reality

- "Getting it all together"

- Being passive or non-emotional

Mindfulness has a passive quality, but it helps you become more engaged with your own life, with your own experiences, and can greatly enrich your life. It isn't some sort of mental trick, nor it is "positive thinking." As Jon Kabat-Zinn (1994) writes: "We can easily become a prisoner of so-called positive thinking. It too can be confining, fragmented, inaccurate, illusory, self-serving and wrong" (95). Mindfulness is about letting go of preconceived notions about self, others, and reality itself. Through its practice you can become increasingly perceptive of things as they are, and more aware of your biases without needing to act in every instance.

In DBT, mindfulness is called *core mindfulness* since it is the core, the hub, around which all the other skills center, intersect, and interrelate. Mindfulness will open the door to other practices such as acceptance and willingness, which I will touch on in later chapters.

The "What" Skills of Mindfulness

Marsha Linehan (1993) writes about "what" and "how" skills of mindfulness. Let's start with the "what" skills.

Observe

Begin by just *noticing* your environment, thoughts, feelings, emotions, and experiences without reacting to them, without judging them. Specifically with your emotions:

- Observe the emotion that you are feeling.

- Just see what is there before you, neither adding to it, nor trying to change it immediately.

- Try to not react to the experience of your emotions. Say to yourself, "I notice that I feel joy/sorrow/love."

- As your thoughts and feelings come and go, slipping in and out, let them. Control your attention, but not what you see. Push nothing away, cling to nothing.

- Be alert to all that comes your way, to every thought and feeling that comes to you.

- Pay attention to the input from your five senses: sight, sound, touch, smell, and taste.

Describe

Now that you have practiced observing, it's time to use words to describe your emotions. Stay descriptive, keeping it all very simple. Don't be troubled if you have difficulty with this at first. If your emotional role models have taught you to ignore or belittle your emotions, you may be very well practiced at being the opposite of attentive and mindful to your own experience.

You can also try some practice statements if you have trouble finding your own voice at first. For example, if this exercise feels unnatural to you, start out by saying to yourself, "I'm noticing that I feel self-conscious right now." If pinning down your thoughts is frustrating to you, say, "My thoughts are coming very quickly just now." Finding your own voice will get easier with practice.

Participate

As a practice to repeat over and over, mindfulness helps you increase the degree to which you participate in your own life and experiences. Through mindfulness you can fully engage in every experience without loving or hating it. Simply participate in each moment as it comes, one moment, then another, staying in the *now* if the moment calls for you to be here now. If you need to plan for your future, then fully participate in planning for your future. Let yourself be a part of what is happening to you without obsessing over it or being overly self-conscious.

Let go of worry thoughts such as "How do I look to others?" or "Am I doing it as well as so-and-so?" Don't focus on concerns about perfection or on performing for others. Give your full attention to the experience here and now. Think of Olympic athletes, who seem so absorbed with their sport or performance, appearing unaware that the world is watching them. They give themselves fully to what they are doing at that moment; they are in their experience.

The "How" Skills of Mindfulness

Now let's look at the ways you practice mindfulness. This involves developing and using "how" skills (Linehan 1993).

Nonjudgmentally

ACTUAL

- See what is actually there—not "shoulds," "musts," the good or right, or the bad or wrong.

- Take your emotions for what they are. Simply accept them as they come.

- Regardless of whether you might consider an emotion to be "good" or "bad," make an effort to look at it without imposing a value upon it.

- The habit of judging is tough to break. Don't be too hard on yourself if it takes time for you to look at your emotions differently.

One-Mindfully

- Focus on one activity, thought, or feeling. It doesn't matter what you are doing as long as you devote yourself entirely to that pursuit. Everyday actions and emotions provide excellent opportunities for the practice of mindfulness.

- Being mindful is not easy, so give yourself a chance and don't give up too soon. When competing thoughts or emotions intrude, gently push them away and return to the subject of your mindfulness exercise. The more often you practice, the more natural mindfulness will feel.

Effectively

- Consider how you want to change and set concrete goals. Keep those goals in view and take actions that will help you to reach them.

- Focus on your current situation—not on what might happen, what you wish would happen, or what you think should happen. The big lesson of mindfulness is that the thing that *is* happening is all that matters.

- Do your best to handle the things that come your way, using your skills wisely and giving each activity your best shot.

- Acting out of anger or doing things just to make a point only hurts you in the end. Holding grudges and dwelling on others' misdeeds, though it may seem satisfying in the moment, will work against you in the long run.

Naming and Describing Your Emotions

Emotion researchers believe that verbalizing emotion is part and parcel of regulating emotions. People who can identify their emotion (be aware) and describe it in a manner that is meaningful to them seem to be better at more quickly reducing negative emotion and stress, and generally regulating their emotions.

As Linehan (1993b) says: "By learning to observe your emotions, you learn to separate from (not identified as) your emotions and at one with your emotions. In order to control, you must be separate from your emotions so that you can think and use coping strategies. But you also need to be one with your emotions, in the sense that you identify them as part of yourself and not something outside you" (89).

To summarize, the rationale applying mindfulness to your emotions includes:

- Learning to be separate from your emotions

- Becoming one with your emotions

- Better controlling your emotions with coping skills (effectiveness)

Naturally, it can be hard to identify and even express an emotion if you lack the words to describe it. To help you build a vocabulary for naming your emotions, see the "Emotion Thesaurus" you'll find in an appendix at the end of this book. Spend some time going over the thesaurus, looking at various synonyms for emotion words. When you see a word that you can identify with, one that really fits with something you have felt before, check the box next to that word. And since I won't necessarily have all of the words that you might identify with, I have left a space where you can add words you might think of. You will also notice that I have added an etymological touch the thesaurus to show where our words come from, as this helps to get the force of a word as it tries to convey emotion. When you have read the thesaurus, you should be better equipped to conduct the mindfulness to emotion exercises.

Beginning Mindfulness to Emotion

Here are a few examples of ways to develop and articulate mindfulness. You will soon develop your own, of course.

When you feel angry

☐ "I notice that my jaw is clenched . . . my hands are balled into fists."

☐ "I observe that I am angry . . . I notice that I feel an urge to stomp my feet."

☐ "I notice that I feel anger toward so-and-so." (Fill in person's name.)

When you feel sad

☐ "I notice that I am avoiding others."

☐ "I observe that I feel empty and drained . . . I notice that I am losing energy."

When you feel joyful

☐ "I observe that I feel like jumping up and down . . . I observe that I am smiling"

☐ "I observe I feel energetic . . . I notice that I have an urge to laugh."

When you feel happy

☐ "I notice that I am laughing . . . I observe that I feel energized."

☐ "I notice a sensation of strength . . . I observe that I feel centered."

When you feel shame

☐ "I observe that I am experiencing shame . . . I notice the urge to avoid the person I disappointed."

☐ "I observe the thought that 'I hate my guts' . . . I notice the desire to apologize."

Now that you have read over these examples, put this book down, sit upright, close your eyes (after you're done reading these instructions), and take one gentle breath. Observe your current thoughts and emotions. What do you notice? Describe what you notice, avoiding judgments about the goodness or badness of what you feel or think. Stay descriptive. When you have finished this basic practice, move on to the following exercise.

A Week of Observing and Describing Emotions

Use the following worksheet to practice observing and describing your emotions. Remember, avoid judgments about the rightness or wrongness of a situation, stick to the facts, stay in the moment that you feel your emotions. They won't kill you, no matter how awful they feel. The following is an example of how to use the mindfulness record. Even if you only practice your mindfulness skills for ten seconds, make a record of that practice, since that will be ten seconds more than you practiced it before picking up this workbook. Be mindful to the full system of emotion, anything that indicates to you that you feel a certain emotion. Make a note about any challenges or distractions you faced during your practice. Make copies of the worksheet, as many as you need.

Observing and Describing Emotions (Example)

Day	Emotion	Observe and Describe Statement	Challenges and Distractions
Mon	Anger	I notice that I am mildly annoyed	Thoughts: this shouldn't happen
Tue	Joy	I notice that joy has filled me	Worried about joy ending
Wed	Fear	I notice butterflies in my stomach	Discomfort with fear and tension
Thu	Anger	I notice that my jaw is clenched	Self-righteousness, desire for vengeance
Fri	Attraction	Heart is pounding, I notice that I have the thought, "I want to kiss my date."	Thoughts about past rejection
Sat			
Sun			

Observing and Describing Emotions

Day	Emotion	Observe and Describe Statement	Challenges and Distractions
Mon			
Tue			
Wed			
Thu			
Fri			
Sat			
Sun			

Mindfulness to Activity Exercises

Read through the following exercises to become familiar with them, then try out the ones that seem most appropriate for you. Follow the directions closely. Some of the exercises will seem somewhat meditative. They will require that you find a quiet place to withdraw to for practice. Other exercises are designed for use in situations where you find yourself being quite active, such as at parties, work, class, on dates, or whatever. Mindfulness is about getting engaged with your life, not becoming a recluse or mystic. Mindfulness is the practice of living more fully and more awake. At the end of each exercise, note any distractions or judgments that came to mind and what you did to go back to the exercise.

These exercises are designed to help you develop basic skills in mindfulness, and may require some time alone. The first group of exercises is built around bringing mindfulness to such everyday activities as eating, driving, shaving, etc. The second group does the same for specific emotions as they come up, such as love, fear, guilt, etc. The exercises are self-contained and carefully structured. (You may find their structure off-putting at first, but surprisingly comfortable later on.) They are certainly formal—but you don't need to rent a tuxedo to do them.

Notes on Mindfulness to Activity

Here is a series of mindfulness exercises you can incorporate into your daily life. For each exercise in this section, write down your thoughts and reactions on the following worksheet. Make as many copies as you need for all of the exercises and any other mindfulness practices you think of and incorporate in your daily life.

What obstacles did you face in doing this exercise? _____

_____

_____

Did your mind wander from the exercise? _____

If your mind did wander, how did you come back to the exercise? _____

_____

_____

If you noticed any judgments about yourself or the exercise, what were they? _____

_____

_____

Mindfulness to Your Body

Lie down on your bed, the floor, or a couch. Take a moment to get comfortable. Lie on your back with your arms slightly away from your body. Take one gentle breath in through your nose, and let it out through your mouth. Simply notice your breath, noticing your belly rise and fall. Close your eyes, bringing your full attention to your body.

Notice how the bed, floor, or couch feels under your body. Is it firm? Is it soft? Are you lying on a smooth sheet or blanket, a coarse rug, or a cool hardwood floor? Give your full attention to the sensations that come to your body, not ignoring anything. What do you notice about how you're supported by what you're lying down on? Stay with the sensations related to lying down, don't let your thoughts wander away from this moment. If the floor feels hard, say to yourself, "I notice the floor feels hard."

Notice where your arms are, what your legs feel, what position your hands are in. If you find yourself judging this exercise, let go of the judgment and come back to this moment; simply notice your judgments and come back to feeling your body stretched out over the bed, floor, or couch. Notice what is happening *now*, not what you wish was happening, or what might happen. If your mind drifts away from this moment, gently bring your attention back to your body and what you're laying on. Bring your attention back again and again and again, as often as you have to during this exercise.

Rationale: Being aware of your body can help you to know when you should seek medical care. It can also help you to rest more fully when you want to relax, by letting go of extraneous thoughts and worries and activities that get in the way of something as simple as laying down.

Mindfulness in the Shower

Start a shower, making the water a pleasantly warm temperature. Getting under the spray of the shower, close your eyes, take in a gentle, centering breath. Focusing just on your breath, bring your full attention to the experience of the shower. Notice everything you feel. Notice the warmth of the water and steam. Be aware of how your body might relax, your muscles softening. Notice your sense of feel, your skin. How is it feeling? What are the smells? Is it just water, or soap, body scrub, or the scent of shampoo?

Keep your mind here in this moment. Live in the shower, just live in this moment. If you begin to think about what happens after the shower, let those thoughts about the future go and come back to this moment, come back to the experience of the shower, experience only the shower. Be fully alive and aware of the shower. If your mind wanders, simply notice that you have wandered, pause, and take a gentle breath to bring your attention back to the shower. If you notice that you're making judgments about your body, the shower, or the exercise, simply notice your judgments, letting them go, come back to this moment. Be in the shower. Practice this for five to ten minutes.

Rationale: As with de-cluttering your rest, you can de-clutter a moment such as a shower so that you can more fully enjoy the experience of the shower or the bath. Mindful showering or bathing brings fullness, richness, to the experience and may help you to increase pleasant experiences. And it is another regular activity that you likely participate in on a daily basis, giving you a chance to more regularly practice mindfulness.

Mindfulness to Shaving

Prepare for your shave. Put out your razor, shaving cream, skin conditioner, whatever you need to shave. Take a gentle, centering breath to bring your attention to this moment, to this practice. As you begin to apply shaving cream or water, notice the sensations that come through your touch, be aware of tactile messages, the feeling of the shaving gel or cream. Notice how these feel on your face or your legs. Be aware of the smells of the gels and creams, the way your skin reacts to warm water. Notice how the razor removes your stubble. If you make a nick or cut here or there, don't judge this event as bad or awful or try to bring it to an end. Simply notice what is happening, do only what is needed. Start to do what is needed by beginning with acceptance of what is, not dwelling on what "should be." As you pull the razor across your legs or face, be very intentional about where the razor goes, be in control of your shaving. Don't attempt to do more than shave. Give your full attention to all that you notice about the shaving, simply describing the experience and all the sensations, being mindful to the experiences of your body.

Rationale: Shaving is a routine activity for most of us, so it provides a chance for mindfulness practice. One becomes practiced at being present and accepting—and of course you may find that when you are intentional about preparation and shaving techniques you suffer fewer nicks and cuts. For those who don't like their faces or bodies, this exercise can be a practice of simple acceptance. If you tend to get very angry when nick yourself as you're getting ready for work, this practice can help you to notice that emotion, perhaps tone it down a bit by accepting this as only *happening*, rather than happening *to you*.

Mindfulness during Exercise

The next time you exercise, be present with your body while you run, stretch, lift weights, or whatever. As you start your exercise, take a moment to clear your mind of anything that isn't essential to your workout. Take a gentle, centering breath, giving your full attention to your breath in order to come to the place you are, being very much aware of your body. If you're running know that you're running, observe and describe, saying to yourself, "I am running . . . I notice my leg muscles flexing and contracting . . . I notice my heart beating faster . . . I notice my breath coming in and out, in and out . . . I notice my breath speeding up . . ." and so on.

If you're lifting weights, pay attention to your form. Be very deliberate and intentional. Notice the feel of the bar in your hand. As you curl the weight, notice your biceps contract. Practice describing the experience of exercise, "I notice my muscles becoming warm . . . I notice that my muscles are becoming tired." If you become distracted by thoughts that you wish to stop, simply notice those thoughts and describe them to yourself, "A thought that I want to quit exercising just entered my mind." Then pause, take in a gentle breath, and bring your attention back to your body and to the exercise. Keep yourself in the present, keep yourself in the exercise, being at home in your body.

Rationale: Being attentive to the sensations of your body during exercise can help you to avoid injury by improving your form. Taking the time to stretch before and after exercise also helps you focus on bodily sensations. Many top athletes and athletic trainers talk about noticing form and letting go of extraneous thoughts during training as the road to better and safer gains.

Mindfulness while Eating

Try this at your very next meal or snack. You can even practice mindful eating without others knowing about it, so if you would like to try it alone first, please do. Sit down to eat and look at your food. Make sure that you're sitting upright, attentive yet comfortable. Don't slouch or hunch over. Take in a gentle centering breath, and bring your full attention to where you are. Take a moment to look over the food, noticing everything about its presentation. Take in the smells of whatever it is that you're eating. Don't just gob the food into your mouth, choking it down. As you pick up your food, by hand or by utensil, take moment to notice its shape, texture, and color. If you're eating finger foods, notice how the food feels in your hands. Is it warm? Is it cold? Is it brown or yellow, or bright red? Let the aroma filter in through your nostrils. Notice your nostrils opening to the smell.

As you take your first bite, begin to chew very slowly, not letting yourself take another bite until you're finished with the first. Chewing intentionally and slowly, make sure that you're only eating. Don't read a book or the paper. Don't look over to-do lists or work-related items. Simply eat. Be attentive only to the activity of eating. If you notice that you begin to work or read while you're eating, simply note that you have begun to do two things instead of just one. Put aside all things unnecessary to eating. If you notice your mind drifting to what will happen at the end of the meal, or if you become focused on how you wish you had a longer meal time, pause, take a centering breath, bring yourself back to eating, one bite at a time, savoring every morsel, being present for every moment of the meal.

Notice what you experience as you eat. Which taste buds water, when you begin to feel satisfied, if you start to feel full or bloated, and what emotions you feel while you eat. Notice what is going on in this moment, and only this moment. Let go of distractions, hurry, or judgments about time, eating habits, and so on.

Rationale: Many of us eat impulsively, eating too much or too little. Mindfulness practice can help you to know what you're eating and when you're eating. It can also help you to truly enjoy what you eat. After all, you aren't just an animal who needs to snarf any old thing down your gullet. You're a human being with the capacity for enjoyment. One final reason for this practice is the fact that many people begin to choke or have their airway obstructed because they didn't chew their food well enough, or they were talking with their mouth full. This practice could well keep you from becoming a choking victim.

Mindfulness to Objects

Taking a few minutes, sit in a chair, upright and attentive but not tense. Placing your hands on your knees, make sure that you're in a symmetrical, balanced, and comfortable position. Once situated, breathe gently in through your nose and out through your mouth, focusing only on your breath. Being centered, look around the room, notice what's in the room with you. Describe to yourself what you see: clocks, chairs, or paintings, whatever is there without adding to it. Don't judge what you see as either pretty or ugly. Stay away from thoughts such as, "My God, why did we buy *that* thing?" If you notice that you're making judgments, let go of your judgments, take another centering breath, come back to the room, and begin again. If you notice your thoughts wandering to tasks or people outside of the room, let go of them and take another centering breath, giving your full attention to where you are at this moment. Stay in this room, be here, simply notice.

Rationale: This practice can help you to become more aware of your environment. Many accidents happen because people aren't paying attention. This can save you from tripping over wires or skateboards, or slipping on banana peels. People who are more aware of their surroundings are less likely to be victims of assault or muggings because they appear alert and confident, and not as easy to surprise or overpower. On the whole the practice helps you to become more alive in your moment-to-moment experience. You become a participant in your own life.

If you're a person who tends to dissociate as a reaction to stress, focusing on objects in your environment can help you to stave off dissociation when you need to be alert and present. That way, you can engage even in stressful situations and stay on top of more of your day-to-day business, while avoiding the sense of being buried.

Mindfulness to Driving

During your next driving trip or commute, do the following. Be fully alert to the fact that you're driving. Before you pull out of your driveway say to yourself, "I am only driving." As you begin to drive to your destination feel the steering wheel in your hands, feel your feet on the gas and brake pedals. Be alert to the other cars on the road. Notice where they are and what they are doing. Don't think about being at work, or at school, or at home. Simply give your full attention to driving. If you notice your thoughts drifting to your destination, or judgments about the other drivers, notice that you have drifted from your practice. Let go of thinking about where you're going since you know where you're going already. Let go of judgments about other drivers. Come back to the present. As you notice emotions arise, just note their presence, not judging them as good or bad. Say, "I notice that anger has just welled up," letting go of any thoughts of driving aggressively or hurriedly, and bring your attention back to driving. Continue to do this over and over and as often as you drive.

Rationale: Being more present and alert as a driver will cut your risk of accidents. If you're quick to get angry when driving, this exercise can help you to simply acknowledge your emotion, without necessarily acting on your impulses or judgments. It can help you to become less impulsive, more intentional, and more tolerant of your emotion.

Mindfulness to Emotion Exercises

Take some time to familiarize yourself with the following exercises. Get a feel for the format as a guide for you to begin your practice of simply noticing your emotions. The more familiar you are with these, the more likely you will remember to practice your observing and describing skills. As I've said, the skill of identifying and labeling your emotions is one of those skills that many emotion researchers agree helps individuals in regulating their emotions.

Mindfulness to Joy

Observe, simply noticing the emotion of joy as it comes. Be attentive to the emotion, neither trying to push it away nor trying to cling to it. Just let the joy come and go naturally.

Describe, putting words on your joy. When joy rises up, say to yourself, "the emotion of joy has just lifted me up," and describe the experience of joy, "I feel light and energetic," or "I feel strong, or connected, or hopeful."

Participate. Fully participate in what is happening, and fully experience your joy. Let go of any ruminating or worry thoughts about when the joy will end. Live presently with your joy while it lasts. As you participate, become one with your joy, become one with the situation, not leaving it mentally. Act intuitively and do only what the situation calls for.

Take a nonjudgmental stance. See only the facts and focus on what is present, not on what you think *should, must,* or *ought* to be going on. Accept your emotion. If you find yourself judging this situation or the emotion, let go of your judging and gently come back to a nonjudgmental stance.

One-mindfully give your full attention simply to the emotion of joy. Feeling joy, just experience joy, not the joy-related sensations and thoughts that may come. Concentrate your mind to make sure you are only doing one thing, and if you notice that you have begun to do two or more activities, simply return to your one activity. Let go of anything that distracts you from your joy or from this moment.

Effectively focus on what works in the situation. Do only what the situation calls for. Don't get hung up on *right versus wrong* or *fair versus unfair* or *should versus should not.* Just do the best you can, keeping your goals in mind. Remember your goals and stay grounded.

Rationale: Sometimes you can cut short moments of joy by getting stuck on thoughts about not deserving to feel joy, or telling yourself, "What's the point of getting into it? It's just going to end." By training your attention on the experience of joy—and letting it come naturally and not pushing it away—you may become more aware of moments in your life when you experience joy, and with increased awareness you can enrich your life by participating in these experiences when they come, and let joy be unfettered by worry or our chattering "monkey mind." Medically speaking, the experience of joy has the potential to help make you more resilient and resistant to the effects of stress. And you'll have more fun in life.

Mindfulness to Anger

Observe, simply noticing the emotion of anger as it comes. Be attentive to the emotion, neither trying to push it away nor trying to cling to it. Just let anger come and go naturally.

Describe, putting words on your anger. When anger rises up, say to yourself, "the emotion of anger has just come alive," or "I notice that I'm agitated," and describe the experience of anger, "I feel tense and aggressive," or "I feel strong, powerful, and hostile."

Participate. Fully participate in what is happening, and fully experience your anger. Let go of any ruminating or worry thoughts about whether or not it's okay to be angry. Live presently with your anger while it lasts. Continue to participate in the moment with your anger, become one with the situation, not leaving it mentally. Act intuitively and do only what the situation calls for.

Take a nonjudgmental stance. See only the facts and focus on what is present, not on what you think *should, must,* or *ought* to be going on. Accept your anger, judging it as neither good or bad, but simply as an emotion that is present. If you find yourself judging this situation or the emotion, let go of your judging and gently come back to a nonjudgmental stance.

One-mindfully give your full attention simply to the emotion of anger. Feeling anger, just experience anger, note all the anger-related sensations and thoughts as they come. Concentrate your mind to make sure you are only doing one thing, and if you notice that you have begun to do two or more activities, simply return to your one activity. Let go of anything that distracts you from this moment. Tolerate your anger. Notice what your anger is telling you, or motivating you toward.

Effectively focus on what works in the situation. Do only what the situation calls for. Don't get hung up on *right versus wrong* or *fair versus unfair* or *should versus should not.* Just do the best you can, keeping your goals in mind. Remember your goals and stay grounded. Don't invalidate your anger as silly or immature, nor as license to really let so-and-so have it. Let go of useless anger and self-righteousness, which will only hurt you.

Rationale: Anger is a troublesome emotion that can lead to everything from unmeant words to crimes of passion. Anger is important, and can motivate you to overcome obstacles, but anger unchecked can lead to impulsive behaviors. In your practice of being mindful to anger you can simply notice its presence, validate it without necessarily acting on it, or be intentional about your anger-based actions. Also, in being aware of anger you will become more skilled at regulating anger, and if you have problems with chronic anger, you can reduce your risk of stress-related illnesses.

Mindfulness to Your Other Emotions

Now that you understand the pattern of the exercise, try the same steps on the other dominant emotions, paying special attention to those that come up most powerfully for you. Here are rationales for love, interest, fear, guilt, and sadness.

Mindfulness to Love

Love as an emotion ranges from that infatuation with a certain someone to a sense of dedication to a person such as a spouse or friend. Love can motivate us to join in relationships with others. Sometimes when you feel love for someone, you may invalidate your feeling for that person by saying, "What's the use, everyone has crapped all over me. They probably will, too" or "My relationships never work out." Even in the cases where the other party, romantic or platonic, doesn't reciprocate, you don't need to enter emotional suffering. If the relationship isn't working out, wait to pronounce it dead when it actually becomes dead, but not sooner. Besides, these thoughts can lead you into secondary emotional responses, derailing you from the present experience of love, and derailing you from moving toward the development of new relationships or the enhancement of existing relationships.

Mindfulness to Interest

One way to develop self-mastery is by participating in learning, whether in formal educational settings, workshops, free lectures, or your own personal research on the Internet or in a local library. Interest can lead you to master a subject in which you can find immeasurable joy, or develop an expertise to take pride in. Interest leads us to find out about people around us and can lead to new relationships or the deepening of existing relationships.

Let go of judgments such as "My ideas are stupid," or "Where am I going with this anyway? No one else cares." Even if others don't care (which they may or may not; you can't be sure), there is your enjoyment and intellectual and social development to pursue, so again, mindfulness can help you cultivate more of what you want in your life, and help you become more self-validating of your interests. Building interests often leads to more enjoyment, potential employment and recognition, and may help in discovering a solution to a problem.

Mindfulness to Fear

Fear gives us important information about situations, perhaps alerting us to real danger, or even social danger. Fear can tell us to stay out of the cars of drunk drivers, avoid foaming doggies, not walk into dark alleys, and so forth. If you judge your fear as weak or pathetic, remember that is your judgment about your fear and not simply fear as an adaptive, primary emotion. Also, if fear becomes all encompassing, it can lead to a number of avoidant behaviors that can wreck your quality of life. People who have been humiliated in social settings may begin by avoiding parties and end up avoiding going out at all or developing agoraphobia. There are many situations in which fear can help us to be careful, but we still need to engage in life.

Mindfulness to Guilt

Why on earth would I want to notice the feeling of guilt? Isn't self-help and therapy about getting over guilt? The answer is both yes and no. There are many writers and experts who divide shame into various categories. Some distinguish between healthy shame and toxic shame, and others talk about shame versus guilt. In the latter case shame is the "bad" emotion and guilt is an appropriate response to actual wrongs. In DBT we talk about *wise mind guilt,* which is close to the idea of guilt that corresponds to actual wrongs against others or your own principals.

Like the other emotions, guilt can alert you to wrongs that you have committed, and prompt you to repair relationships by saying you're sorry or gift-giving—whatever penance would be effective to right the wrong. Guilt is painful and can be a clarion call that we need to change our behaviors. Guilt is usually tied in with social situations. By being mindful to your guilt, you may also discover that you have an over-generalized guilt response in situations that don't call for shame. Simply by noting your shame without judging it, you can engage with others and your life with a growing sense of overcoming a debilitating shame.

Mindfulness to Sadness

Sadness alerts you to loss, and can help tell you what is important to you: your reputation, your family, your pets, or your children. Simply noting your sadness without judging it, you can act as needed, effectively. Perhaps what's effective is temporarily withdrawing from the company of others when your energy is low, or crying on the shoulder of another you can bond with them. Sadness can alert others around you that you need support and care, eliciting help and comfort. Sadness can also alert you to change behaviors about yourself that prompt sadness, say for example by acting in accordance with your personal values, thus helping you to build a sense of integrity.

Keeping a Mindfulness Diary

To keep track of your practice, make copies of the diary card below. Carry it with you in a notebook, put it on your fridge, tape it to your dashboard in your card, or carry it in your purse. Wherever feel like doing a mindfulness exercise, it will be there to help you. The idea behind the card is to help you increase the regularity of your practice, and thereby become more skillful.

On the days that you practice each mindfulness skill (e.g., observe and describe) or specific practice (e.g., mindful driving), circle the corresponding day on the card. As you find yourself trying to increase your practice of mindfulness don't get hung up on whether you did it "completely" or "professionally." If you practice one of the skills for two seconds, then circle that day, since that was probably two seconds more than you have practiced previously. At the bottom there is a place to jot notes regarding obstacles, so that you can become more aware of obstacles to practicing your new mindfulness skills.

Mindfulness Diary Card

Observe	Mon	Tue	Wed	Thu	Fri	Sat	Sun
Describe	Mon	Tue	Wed	Thu	Fri	Sat	Sun
Nonjudgmental	Mon	Tue	Wed	Thu	Fri	Sat	Sun
One-Mindfully	Mon	Tue	Wed	Thu	Fri	Sat	Sun
Participate	Mon	Tue	Wed	Thu	Fri	Sat	Sun
Effectiveness	Mon	Tue	Wed	Thu	Fri	Sat	Sun
Mindful to emotion	Mon	Tue	Wed	Thu	Fri	Sat	Sun
Mindful to eating	Mon	Tue	Wed	Thu	Fri	Sat	Sun
Mindful to driving	Mon	Tue	Wed	Thu	Fri	Sat	Sun
Mindful to exercise	Mon	Tue	Wed	Thu	Fri	Sat	Sun
Other	Mon	Tue	Wed	Thu	Fri	Sat	Sun

Obstacles to mindfulness practice: (Forgetting? Didn't understand skill? Became judgmental? Didn't have card? Others?)

CHAPTER 6

Identifying Your Emotional Triggers

Emotional triggers are events in the outside world and thoughts within you that cause emotions to well up. Triggers are often what people are referring to when they say things like, "That guy makes me so mad," or "That song made me sad." Externally there are things that people say or do to you, traffic, bills, the weather, layoffs, illness, and so on. Within you there are triggers such as remembering, thinking, and ruminating.

Knowing your triggers is a useful step toward dealing with the surges of emotion they can produce. But it's sometimes hard to identify exactly what it is that triggers your feelings. In this chapter, I've listed many events—both external situations and internal thoughts—that people find trigger emotional responses. Which ones apply to you? Pay particular attention to your thoughts, and see if you see any link between your thoughts and your emotions. At the end of the chapter, I'll give you an exercise that can help you build your awareness of those triggers.

Dissociation: Janet

Janet had a serious history of childhood sexual abuse. She had already raised two children who were away at college. She sometimes had flashbacks with past events flooding in on her. These flashbacks, of course, were stressful and frightening, and often triggered dissociative responses that were quite severe. In turn, Janet would engage in cutting herself, which usually ended with her being a little more distressed and at times even ashamed that she had to cut to come back to herself.

DBT's core mindfulness skills specifically target dissociative symptoms. Janet began to practice observing and describing the outcomes of her self-injury in nonjudgmental terms. This gave her the opportunity to see the outcomes of her behavior in a different light and helped reduce her feelings of shame.

Next, Janet became adept at identifying what she felt and experienced before dissociating and blocked her dissociative responses through a myriad of simple yet creative methods—such as holding ice cubes and sucking on frozen strawberries. She found that by letting herself experience some stress, she was able to increase her resilience. Finally, Janet applied her mindfulness skills to triggers in her environment. She educated herself about things that she could change in her environment to decrease her stress, learned to practice accepting things she couldn't change, and used other skills to help her cope.

By paying attention to triggers, by noticing the environment, Janet effectively changed the chain of events that were likely to occur on a given day and applied her DBT skills early in the chain of events rather than being surprised by them. She expressed a new sense of empowerment and mastery, and the last time I communicated with her, she had gone nearly a year without any self-harm.

External Triggers: Situations

Here is a list of outside situations that might trigger emotion.

Love

Situations that trigger love for me include:

- Seeing a beautiful person
- Thinking about my spouse or partner
- Remembering gifts that friends gave me
- Sharing an intimate meal with an attractive person
- Looking at my children
- Watching kids at play

- When I think about how I am loved
- When someone gives me a note of encouragement
- When another person tells me that they love me
- Watching romantic movies
- Watching movies about personal sacrifice
- Sharing a challenging situation with another person
- Thinking about people who support me
- Being with people who know my faults and still accept me
- Thinking that God loves me
- Giving gifts or notes to others
- When I get unsolicited help
- When my therapist, clergy, or doctor gives me encouragement
- Being told that I am smart, good-looking, or a snappy dresser
- Someone tells me, "I love you"
- When someone confides in me

Other: _____

_____

_____

Joy

Situations that trigger joy for me include:

- Hearing beautiful music
- Seeing a baby smile
- Seeing children play
- Holding my baby
- Making love to my partner or spouse
- Thinking of successful times in the past
- Graduating from school, college, or graduate school
- Thinking about God or spiritual matters
- Seeing a sunset
- Eating a delicious meal

- Knowing that my children are safe
- Hearing about a friend's success

Other: _____

_____

_____

Sadness

Situations that trigger sadness for me include:

- Thinking about failures
- Remembering a dear friend or relative who died
- Attending a funeral
- Having a friend or loved one die
- When a friend moves away
- Parents divorce or remembering when they divorced
- Thinking about my own divorce
- Thinking about the divorce of my friends
- Remembering a time when I was ridiculed
- Breaking up with a significant other
- Hearing a song that reminds me of the good old days
- Moving
- When a pet dies or runs away
- My favorite sports team loses an important game
- Losing at games, or remembering times when I did
- Finding out that someone I like likes someone else
- Failing a class
- Being turned down for a job
- Being fired from a job

Other: _____

_____

_____

Fear

Situations that trigger fear for me include:

- Being in crowded places

- Standing at the edge of a cliff

- Driving across bridges

- Driving long distances

- Being alone in the dark

- Hearing about layoffs where I work

- Walking down dark streets

- Being near barking dogs

- Being challenged to a fight

- Having someone stare at me

- Attending parties where I don't really know anyone

- Riding in elevators

- Being a car during a near collision

- Coming across a snake

- Having to speak in public

- Seeing a police car in the rear-view mirror

- Thinking someone will reject me if I ask them out

- Being threatened with bodily harm

- Expecting that someone I love or like will reject me

- When I study for tests

- Thinking about teachers, relatives, or people who have embarrassed me

- When my employer or boss invites me into their office "to talk"

Other: _____

_____

_____

Anger

Situations that trigger anger for me include:

- Hearing someone criticize me

- Getting stuck at a red light or behind a train when I'm already late for work

- When someone challenges my views

- When someone cuts in front of me in the line at the store, bank, or movie theatre

- Being told that I can't have something that I really want

- Finding out that someone has betrayed me

- When I think about my former wife/husband/boyfriend/girlfriend

- When a teacher gives me a grade lower than I deserve

- When I find out that a friend lied to me about something important

- Sitting at an airport at Christmastime and hearing that my flight is canceled

- Being told that I am fired from a job

- Missing a flight, ride, or appointment

- Being stood up for a date or appointment

- Getting a bill for something that I did not buy

- When someone calls my loved one names (kids, spouse, friend, etc.)

- Seeing someone being mean to their pet

Other: _____

_____

_____

Interest

Situations that trigger my interest include:

- Hearing a good book or movie review

- Hearing a friend rave about a product

- Thinking that a subject or person is important

- Thinking that information or a topic will help me understand myself or my family better

- Thinking that knowing something will help me to earn more money or improve my life

- Being told that I need to know something to keep my job

- Believing that certain knowledge will enhance my sense of competence

- Seeing how information, religion, or lifestyle has affected someone else

- Thinking that something is of value to someone important to me

- Thinking that if I know something particular it will help me know more about someone I love

- Being ill

- Seeing something complicated and wondering how it works

- A dear friend or loved one is being affected by something that I study

- Wondering about how cultures are formed

- Asking questions out loud

Other: _____

_____

_____

Guilt

Situations that trigger guilt for me include:

- Breaking something valuable

- Lying to a friend

- Missing an appointment or forgetting about a date

- Saying hurtful words to another person

- Tossing a baseball through my neighbor's window

- When I don't complete homework on time

- Forgetting to pay rent

- Being late to work (again!)

- Forgetting to send a card on someone's important day

- Kissing or flirting with people other than my spouse or partner

- Forgetting to change the cat's litter box

- When I take things that aren't mine

- When I forget that it's my anniversary

- When I make excuses for not giving to charity

- Missing practice for my band or sports team
- Speeding through a school zone
- Refusing to buy Girl Scout cookies
- Hanging up on telemarketers
- Opening another person's mail, accidentally or on purpose

Other: _____

_____

_____

Internal Triggers: Thoughts

Here are some thoughts that might trigger emotion for you.

Love

Thoughts that trigger love for me include:

- Thinking about a person I love
- Thinking that another person loves me
- Thinking about my first kiss, first date, or honeymoon
- Thinking about something nice someone has done for me
- Thinking that love is the most important principle
- Planning to do something loving for another person
- Remembering a gift
- Thinking that another person has my best interest at heart
- Remembering someone who supported me through a tough time
- Remembering "going through something" with a person or certain people
- Remembering being taken care of
- Thinking about someone who stuck up for me

Other: _____

_____

_____

Joy

Thoughts that trigger joy for me include:

- Thinking about beautiful places or things

- Thinking about people who are special to me

- Thinking about my future

- Thinking that other people are wonderful

- Thinking of friends or family as gifts

- Thinking that another's habits are unique

- Remembering a triumph or victory

- Remembering when my child was born

- Thinking about good times

- Thinking about a party or other celebration

- Contemplating sunsets, people, or relationships

Other: _____

_____

_____

Interest

Thoughts that trigger my interest include:

- Wondering how something works

- Thinking that knowledge is power

- Thinking about learning as a tool for a better life

- Thinking that certain information will help get me a raise at work

- Thinking that knowing a subject will bring respect from others in my field

- Thinking that knowing more about a person will help me become more intimate

- Believing that a course will bring self-mastery

- Thinking that spending time with certain people will help me feel better

- Thinking that attending religious services, classes, or workshops will improve my life

- Thinking that having, doing, or knowing something will make life easier

- Remembering when I had fun doing research or going to class

- Remembering excitement that comes with knowing or doing something

Other: _____

_____

_____

Anger

Thoughts that trigger anger for me include:

- Thinking that others' mistakes are intentional slights against me

- Dwelling on past wrongs

- Thinking about evil or injustice

- Thinking about having been swindled, cheated, or betrayed

- Thinking that accidents are intentional events

- Thinking the universe, God, or others are out to get me

- Thinking about someone who stole from me

- Thinking about someone who lied to me or betrayed me

- Thinking my situation is unfair

- Remembering a time when I was angry

- Thinking about something that was kept from me

- Thinking about something I want but can't have, reach, or do

Other: _____

_____

_____

Sadness

Thoughts that trigger sadness for me include:

- Thinking about a loss

- Remembering a breakup with someone I loved

- Thinking about the death of a pet or a person I deeply loved

- Thinking about moving

- Thinking that others don't like me or want me around

- Dwelling on a heartbreak

- Believing that I will never be reunited with loved ones or friends

- Thinking about things that I believe I can never have

- Thinking someone that I like might stop liking me

- Remembering someone I love and have lost contact with

- Thinking about a sad movie that I watched

- Thinking about someone I miss

- Remembering a pet that died

- Thinking about a funeral I attended

- Thinking about a friend or loved one who moved away

Other: _____

_____

_____

Fear

Thoughts that trigger fear for me include:

- Thinking about being stuck in a scary situation

- Thinking I will fail

- Believing or thinking that I am in real danger

- Thinking that I am incapable or incompetent

- Expecting others to reject me

- Believing that I am doomed, or that the world is doomed

- Expecting that a certain person will yell at me

- Thinking I might get fired for a mistake at work

- Thinking about something I can't handle (life, love, work, school, conflict)

- Remembering past times when I was scared

- Thinking about asking for a raise from a difficult boss

- Thinking about choking or looking foolish in public

Other: _____

_____

_____

Shame or Guilt

Thoughts that trigger shame or guilt for me include:

- Thinking about someone that I let down

- Remembering mistakes from my past

- Thinking that I'm stupid

- Attributing my mistakes to stupidity

- Believing that I am a failure

- Thinking about myself as a loser

- Dwelling on embarrassing situations

- Thinking that people hate everything that I do

- Thinking that others think I'm stupid

- Believing that my body (or body part) is ugly or the wrong size

- Dwelling on all of the ways that I have let myself down

- Believing that others are better than I am in most or all ways

- Thinking of myself as unlovable

- Thinking about when people have let me down

- Believing that I never live up to my potential

- Remembering when I lied, stole, or cheated

Other: _____

_____

_____

Making the Connection

As you become skilled at identifying your emotional triggers, you'll be better able to anticipate the emotions they set off. But while external *situations* are relatively easy to identify, the challenge for most people is to identify which of their *thoughts* are emotional triggers.

Commit yourself for one week to make daily records of thoughts that you have, and try to link them to your emotions. See if you can notice the connection between your thoughts and your emotions. Use this worksheet daily, noting the situation, thoughts you had, and what emotions were prompted. Make as many copies of the worksheet as you need.

Knowing Your Thoughts

Day	Situation	Thoughts about the Situation	Emotion
Mon			
Tue			
Wed			
Thu			
Fri			
Sat			
Sun			

The following questions will help you develop your awareness to thought and emotion and their connection. After you read each question, take a moment to write your thoughts.

What patterns do you notice between your thoughts and your emotions? _____

_____

_____

Did you notice a particular "flavor" to your thoughts? (e.g., negative, self-defeating, overly optimistic, etc.?) _____

_____

As you begin to notice patterns and relationships between your thoughts and emotions, what thinking patterns would you like to change? _____

_____

Follow-up: Now that you have completed one week of being mindful to thoughts and emotions and the way they relate to one another, extend your practice from one week to two, then to three, until you notice your awareness becoming more and more second nature.

Remember, these exercises are like training wheels helping you along on a new journey. Just as riding a bicycle eventually becomes second nature, and no longer requires training wheels, as you become more skilled you won't need specific exercises. But you will find that these practices become a lifestyle, a habit, and a part of you. Keep practicing, over and over again.

Chapter 7

Getting the Feel of It:
Urges and Actions

We've been saying that emotion is more than feeling or sentiment—it's at least part action. Once that brain of yours is stimulated and your emotions get activated, your whole body gets involved in some way. So let's talk about those physical sensations and urges associated with various emotions. Bodily sensations can be useful for knowing what emotion you're feeling.

The Feeling of Feelings

When you feel emotions, you also feel your body's readiness for action that matches that emotion. Remember that emotion organizes you to do something. Emotion isn't action per se, but it sets us up for action, prepares us for it. If you feel the emotion of love, for example, what actions might you take? How about anger or shame? Look at the following lists and check the items that you identify with from your experience or memory. As you see, each emotion is paired first with the feelings you might get, then with the actions you might take.

Love

Feelings and urges I experience when I feel love:

- I feel energetic
- I feel invulnerable
- I feel warm
- I feel excited
- I feel relaxed or calm
- I feel aroused
- I feel my heart beat fast
- I feel the urge to call, hug, or kiss the person I love
- I feel secure
- I feel euphoric

Other: _____

_____

_____

Things I do or am likely to do when I feel love:

- I tell others that I love them
- I hug people
- I embrace my partner
- I kiss my partner on the cheek
- I kiss my partner on the mouth
- I give gifts
- I gaze at the one(s) I love
- I hold hands with the one that I love
- I initiate or ask for sex
- I bake goods to give away
- I write poems
- I sing
- I serenade the person I love
- I tell people encouraging statements
- I spend time with those that I love

- I do favors for the people I love
- I do things for people who need them done (errands, lend money, move furniture)

Other: _____

_____

_____

Joy

Feelings and urges I experience when I feel joy:

- I feel light and bouncy
- I want to cry tears of joy
- I have the urge to shout
- I want to be with people I love and care about
- I feel like singing
- I have feelings of euphoria
- I have the urge to run, jump, or dance

Other: _____

_____

_____

Things I do or am likely to do when I feel joy:

- I think about other times I have felt joy
- I think positive thoughts about the future
- I get more tasks done
- I think that everything is OK
- I smile and grin
- I tell others how great things are
- I think positive thoughts
- I walk with a bounce or stride
- I walk upright
- I make more eye contact with others
- I skip along
- I hug people

- I say positive things to others
- I speak with an enthusiastic voice
- I talk a lot, or talk fast
- I write notes of encouragement to other people

Other: _____

_____

_____

Interest

Feelings and urges I experience when I feel interest:

- I have a sense of curiosity
- I want to ask questions
- I feel more focused and concentrated
- I feel clear
- I have the urge to read or study
- I sometimes want to be alone to think, read, study, or learn
- I have a sense of wonder and awe
- I want to spend time alone
- I have the urge to stop doing whatever it is that I'm doing to pursue my interest
- I want to leave work or home
- I feel restless
- I feel distracted or preoccupied

Other: _____

_____

_____

Things I do or am likely to do when I feel interest:

- I study my interest more
- I daydream about the object of my interest
- I ask questions
- I read books
- I watch films, movies, or videos

- I try to find a way to be alone with a person I'm interested in
- I plan time for study, research, or dates for talking with the person of interest
- I do research
- I write papers, books, or articles about my interests
- I talk to experts on my interest
- I tell others about my interest(s)
- I spend time with others who share my interest(s)
- I attend conferences and workshops
- I spend more time at the library
- I pursue activities or join clubs related to my interest(s)
- I collect photos, stamps, books, etc.
- I leave work or home
- I forget to pay bills or attend meetings

Other: _____

_____

_____

Sadness

Feelings and urges I experience when I feel sadness:

- I feel drained
- I have an urge to hide from others
- I want to avoid work, school, and other social settings
- I want to isolate myself
- I feel vulnerable and weak
- I feel lethargic
- My stomach feels tied in knots
- I feel disconnected or unreal
- I want to cry
- I feel raw or crushed
- It feels hard to get out of bed
- I want to think about sad things all day

- My chest feels heavy
- I feel distracted
- I lose my appetite

Other: _____

_____

_____

Things I do or am likely to do when I feel sad:

- I withdraw into my home or room
- I spend more time alone
- I cry, weep, or wail
- I tell others that I'm sad
- I tell others to leave me alone
- I listen to sad music
- I watch sad movies or listen to sad songs
- I stay in bed longer
- I ruminate on what makes me sad
- I focus on my sad emotion
- I question life, myself, others, or God
- I reject attempts by others to comfort me

Other: _____

_____

_____

Anger

Feelings and urges I experience when I feel angry:

- I feel agitated and hostile
- I feel like swearing at everyone
- I feel like hitting pillows or people
- I want to scream at someone
- My muscles are tense and tight
- My brow furls

- My stomach gets tight
- I feel like lashing out at someone or something
- I feel like hiding my anger
- I feel shaky from adrenaline
- My blood boils
- My heart pounds and races

Other: _____

_____

_____

Things I do or am likely to do when I feel angry:

- I frown or grimace
- I throw dirty looks at others
- I yell at others or use a loud voice
- I throw things
- I clench my jaw
- I clench my fists
- I hit pillows or punching bags
- I stamp my feet
- I withdraw from others
- I swear or curse
- I complain more to others
- I tell others that I'm angry
- I avoid the people I'm angry with
- I verbally attack the people I'm angry with
- I stare at people with "dagger eyes"
- I drive more aggressively
- I give people the bird

Other: _____

_____

_____

Fear

Feelings and urges I experience when I feel afraid:

- I feel shaky

- I want to run

- I want to hide

Anger Management: Phil

Phil was a seventeen-year-old young man who was referred to me by the local courts for anger management. He was a normal teenager, attending high school, working a part-time job at a movie theater, playing sports, and trying to get his homework done while pursuing romantic interests. During his first appointment, Phil minimized why the courts had referred him. He said that he was like any other person who got worked up from time to time, but he swore he didn't have an "anger problem."

After a couple of sessions Phil became more relaxed and willing to talk about what things in life triggered his anger. At first, we simply talked about how emotions work by being triggered, then giving him information and organizing him for action. Phil even became open to the idea that he may be a sensitive person. It turned out the reason the courts had referred him is that he attacked one of his parents, and they had reported him to the police.

Phil was actually very pleasant. He was one of these "nice guys" who tried to "let stuff go" if others got on his case, whether friends or family. We discussed the "nice guys" of the world that we read about in newspaper headlines from time to time: "He was such a nice neighbor," or "He always kept to himself," until one day, for whatever reason, he just snapped. I asked if he was one of these nice guys who takes being pushed until he finally snaps. Phil confirmed my hypothesis. Together we agreed that there was a difference between "taking crap" and "letting go." He thought he had been letting go, but as it turned out he was holding on to the way people had pushed him, turning little slights into monumental issues.

He began working on observing and describing what he noticed others doing. He also began to practice breathing exercises and validating his emotional responses to other people and situations. As he began to recognize his emotional responses as legitimate, Phil became more skilled at either genuinely letting go of an irritation, or of identifying it as important and challenging the person with his new interpersonal effectiveness skills. At work, where he received plenty of challenges from a micromanaging boss, he used the distress tolerance skills for brief mental "vacations" by taking his time on his rounds through the theatres while the movies were running. He also practiced his breathing at moments of distress.

Phil still became angry, but he didn't get agitated to the point of combat anymore. He learned to understand and validate his own emotions, and differentiate between "letting go" and "putting up with." He also learned that he could actually become more interpersonally effective and not have to be the sort of nice guy one later reads about in a news headline about homicide.

- I want to escape the situation I'm in
- I feel tense and awkward
- I want someone to take care of me
- I want to stay at home
- My stomach is fluttery with butterflies

Other: _____

_____

_____

Things I do or am likely to do when I feel afraid:

- I avoid people or places that I fear
- I shake or quiver
- I feel short of breath
- I talk nervously
- I cry or whimper
- I plead for help from others
- I run away
- I talk less
- I yell or scream
- I dissociate
- I talk about things that scare me
- I tell others that I'm afraid
- I avoid telling others that I'm afraid
- I pretend that I'm not afraid
- I dwell on things that are scary

Other:_____

_____

_____

Shame

Feelings and urges I experience when I feel shame:

- I feel numb

- I have the urge to run away or flee

- I have the urge to hurt or kill myself

- My gut churns

- My face feels flushed

- I can't talk

- I feel very small or worthless

- My throat feels dry

Other:_____

_____

_____

Things I do or am likely to do when I feel shame:

- I hide from others

- I hang my head low

- I shuffle when I walk

- I ask for forgiveness

- I become apologetic

- I become overly apologetic

- I say I'm sorry

- I slump more

- I give gifts to "make it up" to others

- I try to fix damage I think I've done

- I dwell on my failures

- I tell others how worthless I am

- I keep my eyes down

Other:_____

_____

_____

In this chapter we worked on showing how the body gets involved in stimulating emotion and responding to it. In the next chapter, we'll focus on the consequences of that emotion—emotional fallout.

CHAPTER 8

Emotional Fallout

In DBT, we like to say, "Emotions love themselves." That is, once an emotion is activated, it organizes the person's mind and body in such a way as to continue the same emotion. So when an emotion is fired up, that same emotion tends to re-fire again and again. Fortunately, I can teach you some specific skills to break these constantly cycling emotional states. The skills, which fall under the heading of *opposite action*, involve engaging in motor behaviors that are incompatible with the current emotion. We'll cover them in chapter 11.

For now, I'd like you to continue building awareness to the way that specific situations affect you, your emotions, and the outcomes of your actions. I'm going to ask you to use a worksheet every day for a one week to describe the outcomes of behaviors that you engage in. It will help build your awareness to the outcomes of your behaviors and hopefully reveal to you the effectiveness of certain behaviors as related to your goals. Later you will use a complementary worksheet that includes a section on what you might do differently next time.

Here is what a completed worksheet might look like:

Emotional Fallout (Example)

Day	Event	Emotion	My Action(s)	Fallout	Effec- tiveness (0-100)
Mon	I got stuck behind a train on my way to work	Anxiety	Muttered some swear words	Felt more anxious & angry	0
Tue	Got stuck behind train again	Anxiety	Turned on radio and sang loudly	Felt a little less anxious	50
Wed	Boss talked to me about being late to work	Embar- rassment	Apologized for being late and promised to cor- rect problem	Boss expressed gratitude, to my surprise	75
Thu	Cat's leg got caught under rocking chair	Fear & panic	Drove cat to vet, swearing all the way	Felt angry, was curt with clinic staff. Later felt stupid for overreacting	30
Fri	I asked Suzy out for a date and she said yes	Elation & happiness	I told friends about date, smiled a lot	Felt energized and excited, daydreaming	75
Sat	Suzy called and thanked me for a fun date	Excited	Cracked jokes and schmoozed with Suzy	I asked Suzy out again, she said yes	100
Sun	Hung out at bookstore all day	Relaxed	Read, thought about Suzy, drank coffee	Felt rested and positive, ready to face work again	100

Now here is a blank worksheet for you to use. In the fallout area write about what your emotions are like after you have acted in a situation and comment on how things were made worse or better, or how they stayed the same. In the effectiveness section comment on how effective your behavior was with respect to how closely it aligned with your goal in this situation or your values. Use a scale of 0 through 100 (0 = extremely ineffective, 100 = highly effective). After you complete this for one week, do it for another week, and so on—just one week at a time. Make copies of this worksheet so you have plenty on hand for future use.

Emotional Fallout

Day	Event	Emotion	My Action(s)	Fallout	Effectiveness (0-100)
Mon					
Tues					
Wed					
Thu					
Fri					
Sat					
Sun					

Acceptance: Phyllis Lives with Her Anger

Phyllis was a sensitive person, well educated, musical and creative, and the mother of a two-year-old boy. She was also was easily angered—not by others, but usually by herself or what she saw as her own failings. At times she got so angry she would hit her legs out of sheer frustration.

Phyllis had been in therapy for several months when she had a "meltdown" at home one evening. She had been feeling frustrated and went to play games on her computer, which she used to distract herself. She was already agitated, and was counting on playing the computer games, a strategy she learned with her distress tolerance skills. To her dismay, the computer had frozen up. She tried rebooting the computer, but it kept on crashing. As Phyllis continued this cycle, tears welled up her eyes and she could feel herself becoming more and more angry. She noticed her thoughts, "Why now?" and "I'm trying to be skillful, and this is what I get?"

At that point, her husband came to her aid. In a soothing voice, he asked if he could help her, especially help her feel better. This was a scenario they had played out a thousand times in their marriage. But this time, Phyllis kindly thanked her husband for trying to be helpful. Then she told him, "How can I learn to live with my anger, until I start living with my anger?" You see, Phyllis recognized that to better tolerate her anger, she had to let herself feel her anger and simply accept it as it comes and goes; neither pushing it away, nor clinging to it, and certainly not judging it as awful. That night, she made a strategic choice that made a world of difference for her.

It also made a difference to some of my other clients, to whom she told this story in a group session. Some began to adopt this approach with an array of emotions that were giving them trouble. The new mantras were, "How can I live my fears until I start living with my fears?" or "How can I ever live with my anxiety until I let myself live with my anxiety?" It became an excellent tool for practicing nonjudgmental exposure to emotion.

Observing Your Fallout

Use the worksheet below to elaborate your observations about events, emotions, urges, and actions taken in specific situations that make you feel emotional. (Example: "My supervisor asked to see me about a problem that I may have caused.") You might want to take some of the entries from your diary sheet in chapter 6 and plug them into the worksheet. Make copies of the blank worksheet so that you can use it for as many different situations as you can think of.

Emotional Fallout Record

Event or situation: _____

_____

What I was thinking: _____

_____

Emotions that I experienced: _____

_____

Action urges I experienced: _____

_____

My actions: _____

_____

Fallout and consequences: _____

_____

Examples of fallout:

I feel more masterful over myself

I feel more out of control

I feel less masterful over myself

What are your feelings about other people involved?

Examples:

Feelings of regret

More angry, sad, or anxious than before

I have made a relationship worse

I must engage in relationship repair

Things were made worse

I feel low

I feel more powerful

This situation can't be repaired

Learning from Fallout

Emotional fallout, or the consequences of strong emotion or particular behaviors, may be positive or negative. Use the following worksheet to articulate how the emotional fallout was negative (an obstacle and difficult to overcome) or positive (i.e., it helped you bond with another person). If nothing else, you can always learn from these situations and from the fallout. This is very important, since emotions can help you change problematic behavioral patterns. But you have to pay attention to get the feedback that comes from the fallout. This is what makes knowing and remembering so vital to you, and of course, what makes mindfulness so important

Learning from Fallout

Describe the situation, including who and where, that triggered your emotions:

_____

_____

Describe your thoughts at that time: _____

_____

_____

Describe your emotions at that time: _____

_____

_____

Describe your actions: _____

_____

_____

Describe the fallout in terms of continued emotion, new emotion, relationship strain or improvement, etc.: _____

_____

_____

What did you learn from the situation? _____

_____

_____

What might you do differently the next time you're in a similar situation? _____

_____

_____

In this and earlier chapters we discussed the role of thought in the life of the emotions and how *thinking* can intensify or regulate emotions. In the next section of the book, we'll look more broadly at the ways your *actions* affect your emotions, and how those actions can be changed in order to shape the emotions. We'll start with the emotional effect of the demands you make of yourself, the world, and others.

PART III

Reducing Blocks to Emotion Regulation

CHAPTER 9

Challenging Your Self-Talk

We all hold assumptions about how things are supposed to be and work. We all have a sense of right and wrong, and we know that we want to be treated a certain way. And that's fine. What can become a problem are thinking patterns that are inflexible or rigid. (Those include the "top five" automatic thoughts and beliefs you identified in chapter 4.) This is also called *dichotomous* thinking, which you can define as either-or or all-or-nothing thinking.

If you hold a belief about how you should be treated, but others around you don't treat you that way, you may feel angry, sad, or afraid. It isn't wrong to want to be treated a certain way, but if you stubbornly cling to your expectations without accepting the reality that you aren't always going to be treated that way, you'll experience unnecessary emotional suffering.

As we've discussed, thoughts can trigger emotion. If you remember a date that went well, you will feel joy and warmth, and maybe smile. If you remember one that went poorly, you may feel sadness, or maybe embarrassment about being clumsy or being treated coldly. Even after a thought triggers emotion, subsequent thoughts can keep triggering the same emotion, or they can trigger secondary emotional responses. However, if you open your mind to the inevitability of pain and disappointment, you'll find yourself able to regulate your emotions a bit more quickly, or at least realize that even a bad experience isn't necessarily a total wash.

As you work through the exercises in this chapter, you'll notice that I'm casting a pretty wide net when I talk about self-talk. Under the heading of thought I include automatic thoughts, beliefs, hidden philosophies, self-talk, or what are sometimes referred to as "tapes" that have been recorded into our brains. Whatever we call them, all these aspects of thought affect your emotions.

Automatic Thoughts That Affect Emotion

Here are some examples of unbidden thoughts that can affect emotion. Notice how charged many of them are.

- I should never feel angry/sad/scared
- It's bad to be emotional
- Showing emotions is a sign of weakness
- I should always be happy and feel good
- I can't stand it when I feel lonely
- I should always feel love toward others
- I should always be upbeat
- If I'm sad, I have a bad attitude

The above thoughts represent beliefs about emotion per se, but we also hold beliefs about all sorts of aspects of social well-being. In their 1990 book *A Primer on Rational-Emotive Therapy*, Windy Dryden and Raymond DiGiuseppe structure "musts" into three basic categories: demands about self, demands about others, and demands about world/life conditions.

Looking at the three kinds of demands below, do any ring true for you? If so, check those statements that reflect your own automatic thoughts, then use the blank lines below to list any of your other automatic thoughts. Finally, put on your dialectical hat and try to come up with at least one challenge to each of the thoughts you checked:

1. Your demands on yourself

Check the demands that you identify with and then rate the strength with which you hold this belief (0 = not at all, 100 = absolutely):

- ☐ I must do well in everything I put my hand to, and if I don't, it's awful _____
- ☐ I must be approved of by all significant others in my life, and its awful if I'm not _____
- ☐ I'm not lovable if I fail at this important task _____
- ☐ I'm a damnable person if I'm not loved or don't do well _____
- ☐ No one will like me if I'm not competent at everything I do _____
- ☐ I must be a loving person at all times, and to all people _____

☐ I must never tell others that I'm angry ____

☐ I must always be in total control of my emotions and behavior ____

Other: _____

2. Your demands on others

☐ Others must treat me justly and fairly ____

☐ I can't stand it when others treat me badly or shabbily ____

☐ When others treat me poorly, they deserve to be punished ____

☐ When others don't give me what I want, they must pay for it ____

☐ If people do what they shouldn't, then they're bad or evil ____

☐ I can't like others who let me down ____

☐ It's a disaster when I don't get what I want from others ____

Other: _____

3. Your demands about the world or life conditions

☐ Life should always be easy and carefree ____

☐ I can't stand challenges in life ____

☐ There should never be any pain ____

☐ It's not fair when things don't go my way ____

☐ If I'm good, the world (or God, or the universe) should treat me well ____

Other: _____

Are You *Shoulding* on Yourself?

Now let me introduce you to another pattern of thought that may be giving you problems: *shoulding* on yourself. This is a concept central to Rational Emotive Behavior Therapy (REBT), a therapy first articulated by psychiatrist Albert Ellis in 1955.

We've seen how *shoulds* can affect your outlook, mood, and emotional states. But it's useful to distinguish between shoulds of a logical necessity, and social shoulds. Because when social shoulds are rigid, inflexible, and over-demanding, they can cause you suffering. Challenging those social shoulds can reduce that suffering or free you from it.

Shoulds of logical necessity are phenomena that work the way we expect them to because of laws that we neither cause nor affect. For example, if I drop a water balloon from the roof of a building, the balloon should fall, because of gravity, and it should break open with a splash. When we go to bed at night, the sun should rise the next morning, because the Earth is spinning on its axis. How you feel about those facts doesn't affect them one way or another; the balloon will burst and the sun will rise anyway.

Social shoulds are very different, and getting too attached to them can cause you a lot of distress. Society has shared moral codes and social mores, but people are people, not machines. They aren't balloons, and they aren't sunrises. As a result, while they have many behaviors that are reliable and predictable, they also often do things they shouldn't. They let you down, they do you wrong, and sometimes they just goof up. Even when they don't mean to do you wrong, they sometimes manage to hurt you anyway.

If you have a sense of being wronged, your shoulds have been violated. That's not bad in and of itself. In fact, some of those shoulds are related to your basic values, and I wouldn't change them unless I had a very good, personally important reason. But if you rigidly expect people and life to treat you just so—and always fairly and well, of course— you'll experience more than your share of disappointment.

Should People Signal?

Let's look at driving, a common situation that is rife with shoulds. Question: Should drivers use their turn signals when turning or changing lanes? Well, yes and no. They should use their signals because it's the law. They should use their turn signals so cops won't give them tickets for failing to signal properly. We could also say that drivers should signal in order to let you and other drivers know what they're planning to do, which makes for safe driving. (Did you notice how we've shifted from an isolated to a social situation?)

Now let's suppose that you're on the road, another driver fails to signal a turn, and you get very angry. It's most likely because you have the automatic thought that they should use their signals, and that they're idiots for being so intentionally inconsiderate. Shoulding on yourself also seems to have an element of judgment about intent. "So-and-so shouldn't do such-and-such" or simply, "They should know better!"

If you have deep, rigid, and inflexible expectations that people should be or act a certain way, you'll be terribly upset—in fact, you'll should yourself right into a corner of suffering. Challenging your shoulding isn't just about letting others off the hook for what they do, and it doesn't require that you give up important moral values of your own. Challenging your shoulding behaviors will first and foremost help you keep yourself out of that corner of suffering.

Recording Your Self-Talk and Judgments

The following exercise will help you become increasingly aware of your self-talk, particularly those shoulds and their connection with the way you experience your emotions. Starting with just one event daily, complete this exercise for an entire week. Try to note at least one daily event and any shoulds that you notice, then rate the accompanying emotion and the strength of that emotion. I'll give you a sample worksheet of self-talk and judgments, then a blank one for you to use (and copy).

A Self-Talk and Judgments Diary (Example)

Day	Event	Should(s)	Emotion (Rate: 0-100)
Mon	Driving, got cut off by another driver	This should never happen, people shouldn't drive that way	Anger (60)
Tue	Boss yelled at me in front of coworkers	People should never do this kind of thing ever, people should always show respect	Embarrass-ment (100)
Wed	Thought about yester-day when boss yelled at me	I should be competent in everything that I do	Guilt (50)
Thu	My children didn't say thanks for their new toys	People should always thank you for gifts, especially children	Anger (50)
Fri	Coworker asked me about what happened on Wednesday with boss	People should never ask a person about an embarrass-ing situation	Anger (70)
Sat			
Sun			

A Self-Talk and Judgments Diary

Day	Event	Should(s)	Emotion (Rate: 0-100)
Mon			
Tue			
Wed			
Thu			
Fri			
Sat			
Sun			

Dialectical versus Dichotomous Thinking

To understand a dialectical framework, think of the polarities inherent in reality, the many opposites we encounter in daily life and the way things work. From the simplicity of night and day to the unseen tension between matter and antimatter, reality is full of opposites. There is both day and night, not one or the other.

Dialectical thinking presupposes that a thesis ("Expressing emotions is good") will confront its antithesis ("Controlling emotions is good"), and that over time the two will synthesize ("Expressing and controlling emotions are both good").

In contrast, *dichotomous* thinking is all-or-nothing, black-or-white thinking. It's also a kind of trap. On the one hand, you think you should be able to control your emotions. On the other hand you think you should be able to express you emotions. Which proposition is true? Is one true at the expense of the other?

Remember when we discussed making rigid demands on yourself, others, and the world? Those are examples of dichotomous thinking. If you believe that either you have to be amazingly competent in every situation or you're a miserable failure, you are thinking in black-or-white dichotomies.

Dialectical thinking is more flexible and open to the synthesis of opposites (or apparent opposites), which is often the way life is. We're often confronted with paradox, and there isn't always an obvious synthesis between opposites. This is where dialectical thinking can be helpful.

Here's a dialectical way to look at your belief about being competent. If you weren't as competent as you would have liked at a given moment, that only means that you didn't perform as well as you wanted to at that moment and at that specific task, not that you're a failure, essentially and metaphysically in every respect and the very core of your being.

Dialectical thinking is also a matter of finding a middle path between extremes—extremes of emotion (stuffing versus overreaction), thinking (black or white versus black and white), or relationships (They either love me or hate me, rather than they both love and hate me).

To sum up, dialectical thinking:

- Is flexible

- Is synergistic/holistic

- Asks, "What's being left out?"

- Asks, "Where can we put the *and*?"

When you're confronted with apparent contradictions or conflict, try using dialectical thinking. With help from your mindfulness skills, try to turn towards tolerance for differences of opinions. In the case of interpersonal conflict, let others set their own personal limits while you set yours, knowing that limits can fluctuate from time to time and don't have to be fixed. Life isn't all or nothing. It's usually both/and.

Self-Invalidation

In chapter 4, we talked about contributing factors that make emotions hurt more than they have to. One of those factors is growing up or living in an invalidating environment, internalizing those invalidating messages, and carrying them with you to this day. *Self-invalidation* can activate secondary emotions and impede effective behaviors. Because it also keeps you from taking your own challenges seriously, it can lead you to minimize the difficulty entailed in changing habits and patterns.

Self-invalidation often shows up when someone is trying to quit a bad habit, such as smoking, drinking, or overeating. Let's say a woman you know is determined to quit smoking, but has a lapse and smokes a cigarette or two. In confessing the lapse, she says, "Well, it's because I was hanging out with Joanie. I've got it out of my system now. No worries." Let's imagine this woman has been smoking for ten years. Smoking is a highly addictive behavior with many triggers, memories, and pleasures connected to it. What the woman needs is to become aware of what triggers her smoking. That way, she can plan how to resist the urges through alternate behaviors, thought stopping, and so on. Just saying, "It's over," is magical thinking. It isn't taking the challenge seriously.

Acknowledging that your challenges are real and important—and sometimes difficult—is to validate your experiences and yourself. In the next exercise, you will practice *validating yourself* with statements that reflect taking your problems seriously.

Here are some examples of self-validating statements:

- I have good reasons for being emotional, even when others don't agree.

- My ineffective patterns have been a long time in the making, and they'll require a lot of work to change.

- Change is tough.

- When I feel hurt I want to cry.

- When I feel hungry, I'm hungry.

- I am going to have to get help to overcome certain problems.

Use the following worksheet to describe the habits you're trying to change, and list the statements you might make that invalidate and validate your efforts.

Moving beyond Invalidation

Describe the habit or behavior you are trying to change: _____

_____

Invalidating responses:

- It shouldn't be so hard.

- I should be past this already.

- I'm just dumb/lazy/worthless.

- It's no big deal (minimizing). It won't happen again.

Other: _____

Describe how these limit you: _____

_____

Validating responses:

- This situation/habit is hard for me to change/quit.

- I may get past this, but it will take time and practice.

- This situation/habit is important for me to change.

- My emotions about the situation/habit can help me to change.

Other: _____

What do you find challenging in validating your responses? _____

_____

_____

Now let's try something a little different. Begin by describing some situation that you find difficult and in which you experience distress. Try to think of situations that are likely to trigger self-invalidating thoughts and statements. It may revolve around a habit you are trying to break or dealing with a certain person.

In what way do your current responses and reactions to the situation make sense when you think about your own skills or your history with this problem ("No one ever showed me another way," "I don't know what I'm doing," "My responses are inappropriate, but they get me what I want in the end")?

Self-Validation to Overcome Difficulty

Describe a situation that you find difficult or have experienced many times: _____

_____

Based on your history and your present skills, how does your current behavior, and difficulty, in this situation make sense? _____

_____

Write out specific statements of self-validation: _____

_____

Although your current responses make sense, describe what you like would like to be different or how you would like to change: _____

_____

Self-Validation That Stresses the Positive

Describe the situation: _____

_____

Label the primary emotions you feel in this situation: _____

_____

How do your current behaviors make sense in this situation? _____

_____

Describe your capabilities and describe what you do right, well, or effectively, so far in this situation: _____

_____

Describe what it would be like to trust your own primary emotion responses to this situation: _____

_____

Describe your commitment to try to act from primary emotion the next time you face this situation: _____

_____

Describe the best aspect of your efforts, motivation, and goals in this situation: _____

_____

Moving On and Out

Now that we've looked at the way we can start to get control over our emotions from the inside, it's time to look outward. In the next chapter, we'll explore how making changes in our lifestyles can help us manage our emotions. Among other things, we'll look at the effects of caffeine, sleep, eating, and exercise, and explore ways to get and stay healthy, have fun, and be mindful of pleasure.

CHAPTER 10

Lifestyle Changes for Emotional Resilience

In this chapter we'll consider what factors tend to make you more reactive or more vulnerable to intense emotional dysregulation. Many of them affect your body, and since emotions are hard-wired biologically, they will have a direct effect on your emotions. Factors such as rest, hydration, and nutrition can have a big effect—both positive and negative—on your emotions, so it's important to pay attention to lifestyle habits.

I'll be covering pretty commonsense material, and I'm presenting it here mainly to remind you of what you already know. It doesn't take a genius to realize that if we eat properly and get plenty or exercise and sleep we'll feel better and have a better handle on our emotions. If we have varied and rewarding relationships, we'll have sympathetic ears and helping hands available. If we take time to have fun, we'll feel better.

As I said, it doesn't take a genius. But the material below may include some tips and ideas that you hadn't thought of, and I hope you find them helpful. Later in the chapter, we'll talk about setting out to find small pleasures that can bring some healing and laughter.

Let's start with lifestyle habits that can make you exceptionally vulnerable to being too emotional, and in turn make you impulsive or reactive. Take a moment to look over the following list, and check all the factors that are relevant to you.

Factors that increase vulnerability to being too emotional include:

☐ Too much caffeine

☐ Too much alcohol

☐ Sleep problems

☐ Junk food

☐ Candy and sweets

☐ Isolation

☐ Sedentary life or work, lack of exercise

☐ Overeating

☐ Under eating

☐ Other: _____

_____

_____

In a moment, I'll share some thoughts about food and drink, and exercise and sleeping, since these are all under our control and can have a big impact on our emotions. But I better start with a confession. Coffee is one of my great loves, and suggesting that anyone should cut down on it made this one of the hardest parts of the book for me to write. I'll be honest: Americanos, almond lattes, breves, cappuccinos, and good dark-roasted coffees—I love them all. (I also love potato chips, but that's another topic.) What matters is that I try to keep that love under control. So do as I say, not as I brew.

Caffeine

Caffeine is a good pick-me-up in the morning, and if you work the night shift it can become your lifeblood. But when used to excess, caffeine acts as a diuretic and can dehydrate you. Also, it suppresses appetite and interferes with your body's usual signals to eat, which can lead to undernourishment or malnourishment. Not eating can lead to imbalanced blood sugar levels, which can impair mental and physical performance and lead to general agitation.

Too much caffeine can aggravate heart conditions and anxiety-related symptoms like racing heart, pressured speech, shaking, and racing thoughts. Depending on your sensitivity, it may trigger insomnia or interfere with restful sleep and so contribute to general fatigue. People who need to relax, gain weight, or sleep should really stay away from caffeine.

Illness

Illnesses can make you more reactive and agitated or exacerbate symptoms related to mental disorders and other medical conditions. So see your physician, take his or her advice, get plenty of rest, and drink lots of water. Depending on the illness, however, don't move too quickly back to your usual pace. Last winter I had a bout with viral pneumonia that came with such fun symptoms as profound weakness and shortness of breath. My recovery entailed mostly rest and loads of water, along with a temporary inhaler to open my lungs. After I began to feel better I increased my exercise to my pre-pneumonia baseline and, *wham!* I was back down with major fatigue. I had to pace myself.

You may find that when you change some of the other areas described in this chapter, you'll have fewer minor illnesses. Than can mean less time away from work or school, which in turn could mean less isolation and less falling behind with important work, which can be a major source of stress.

Exercise

Exercise helps me in many ways. On days that I exercise I notice that I have increased energy, my mood is much better and positive, and I can focus better. Because of my schedule I exercise in the morning, and it sets a great tone for the day. On days that I don't work out I feel a little more flappable and unbalanced, and my vulnerability to stress and discombobulation is greater.

Researchers have found a correlation between physical and mental and emotional health and strength. This doesn't mean that if you exercise six hours a day you can be guaranteed optimal mental and emotional health. Actually, too much exercise can become pathological and all consuming, and can lead to eating disorders, social isolation, and body dysmorphic disorder.

We need to exercise our bodies for strength, endurance, and flexibility. Strength training—weight lifting, for example—slows muscular atrophy, the process by which muscles shrink. Resistance training can increase bone density, which in later life helps avoid osteoporosis. Strength training is associated with increased libido and the production of testosterone, which is especially important for men as they age, and reduced instances of adult-onset diabetes, obesity, heart disease, hypertension, and arthritis.

Endurance training strengthens the heart and facilitates the transport of oxygen cells throughout your body, and helps reduce fat levels by converting fat into fuel for exercise. Cardiovascular exercise can help you to feel refreshed and alert, and is associated with improved memory and learning. It has long been known that cardiovascular exercise reduces stress, probably because it keeps fat levels down and reduces "bad" cholesterol in your arteries.

Stretching keeps tendons and muscles flexible and helps joints and muscles maintain a full range of motion. Also, it feels good and can have a soothing effect. But don't wait for exercise to stretch. If you do a lot of sitting for your job or studies, get up and stretch often during the day. Your body will get some badly needed stress relief, especially if you do a lot of typing or other repetitive activity that uses fine motor skills.

Guidelines to Better Exercise

● First, get a physical examination. This will be important if you have any pre-existing health problems that can be exacerbated by exercise or particular kinds of exercise. Be sure to follow any additional guidelines provided by your physician.

- As you make plans to exercise, start with small, achievable goals. For example, decide that you will exercise two or three days per week for at least twenty minutes. Let go of unrealistic expectations. Don't expect to be buff and ripped after only a week or even a month of exercise.

- Get an exercise partner. Whenever I have someone to work out with I am more regular. Your partner should be someone with whom you can make mutual and reciprocal commitments to stay true to your exercise programs.

- Choose exercises that you can actually do and have the equipment to do. Choose exercises that you enjoy.

- Don't overdo your exercise at the beginning. This can be troublesome for ex-athletes, who can remember a time when they could run for miles and lift weights by the ton. Break your muscles in gently. Consistency is the key to getting the benefits of exercise.

- Make sure that your exercises are providing training for strength, flexibility, and endurance. Drink plenty of water before, during, and after exercise. Include warm-up and cooldown periods in your exercise routine.

- Take up a recreational sport to make exercise fun. Go hiking with friends, play volleyball or softball, try bowling, play badminton, and so on. Schedule your exercise time. If you don't schedule periods for exercise you're less likely to actually exercise. Whether it's 4:30 A.M., lunchtime, or in the evening, do whatever works.

- Reinforce your exercise behaviors. Give yourself a present—a new book or CD, say—after you do three or six workouts. Go for a massage after two months. Use reinforcers that are meaningful to you and will help strengthen patterns of exercise and your motivation.

- Practice mindfulness as you exercise. Being intentional helps avoid injuries and increases athletic gains or performance.

Rest and Sleep

One of our most common complaints these days is that we don't get enough sleep. Throughout the day we are stressed. Not in a pathological way, just generally. Our bodies are stressed by simply being awake and tending to daily activities. Deep and restful sleep is restorative of energy. Rest is a key element in making gains related to exercise since it is during rest that muscles repair from the stress of exercise.

Good Sleep Hygiene

Follow these guidelines to get a better night's sleep and rest:

- Get at least twenty minutes of vigorous exercise every day.

- Don't use alcohol to sleep. Alcohol blocks REM sleep, which you need. Avoid caffeinated beverages after noon. You may want to stop even earlier if your body is especially sensitive to caffeine.

- Don't eat, read, or watch television in your bedroom. Your body may come to associate your bed with these activities instead of sleeping.

- If you don't fall asleep right away, get out of bed and go to another room to read or listen to soothing music. If you stay in bed while feeling alert your body may associate feelings of alertness or agitation with your bed or bedroom. Go back to bed when you again feel sleepy.

- Don't judge or react to your wakefulness. If you begin to judge this situation and react strongly to it as awful, you may activate strong emotions not associated with rest, such as anger or anxiety.

- Practice diaphragmatic or belly breathing. Sit or lie down somewhere you can allow yourself to breathe easily. Begin with three centering breaths giving your full attention to the breath as it enters gently, and when it leaves your body.

- If you can't sleep but feel tired and agitated, lie down on your back on your couch or a comfortable floor. Then place a damp washcloth or hand towel over your eyes. Fold the cloth so that it doesn't block your mouth or your nose. The cloth will keep your eyes closed, affording your brain a bit of rest from visual stimulation. Play some soothing music, preferably with the lights off, but if you want some light either burn a candle or keep a nightlight on. Everything about your environment should be soothing and restful.

- Take a very hot shower or bath. Drink warm milk; it contains tryptophan, a chemical that is known to elicit a relaxation response in the body.

- Avoid thinking about disturbing things or memories. Stay away from late-night problem solving, especially at 3 and 4 o'clock in the morning when you can't effectively do much about your problems anyway. If you have difficult subjects on your mind, take a moment to write out a list of your concerns. But leave them on the list and go to sleep. They'll be there in the morning for you to be concerned about.

- Set your alarm for the time you want to get up in the morning. Get up no matter how little sleep you got. This is the best way to start regulating your sleep. You can't force yourself to go to sleep, but you can force yourself awake. Waking up every day at a regular time has been one of the most effective means for treating insomnia and other sleep disturbances.

- If you have extended periods of sleep disturbance or believe you might have a sleep disorder, see your physician for referral to a specialist. Sleep disorders respond well to cognitive-behavioral therapies.

Religion and Spirituality

A growing body of research literature supports the idea that religion and spirituality are good for people. Why is that? On a very practical level, people who are religious or spiritual tend to have fewer bad habits than their secular counterparts. Many religious and spiritual groups frown on smoking, alcohol, and overeating, for example. This puts these folks at lower risk for health problems associated with cancer, alcoholism, and heart disease. Furthermore, religiously and spiritually committed individuals are likely to report healthy and supportive relationships in their respective communities of faith, again taking us back to the protective quality that relationships can afford us. Prayer, meditation, and worship have been shown to correlate with lowered reported stress, probably because they provide relaxation and coping mechanisms. Finally, religion and spirituality give people hope and a reason for living, which helps them better endure life's hardships.

What if you don't consider yourself religious or spiritual? You can still practice meditation and mindfulness. And getting connected to a cause or community that shares a common task or mission that is bigger than you can provide you with some of the same benefits as religious and spiritual communities.

Increasing Positive Emotions

All right, let's say we've done it all. We quit smoking, sleep eight hours a night, exercise regularly, drink plenty of water, and chant "om" until our alpha brainwaves are as calm as an alpine lake. What should we now? We have fun; it's doctor's orders.

Take time to see movies, go for walks, go dancing, try new things, or attend book clubs, writers' groups, or religious and spiritual services. By intentionally engaging in events and activities that you find enjoyable, you activate hormones related to a sense of well-being, like endorphins and serotonin. This is in part why persons suffering from depression do better when they increase their activities and exercise, especially when these activities take them outside of their homes.

Understanding Fun

1. Describe your idea of fun: _____

_____

_____

2. How did your parents model fun for you? _____

_____

_____

3. What obstacles are in your way when you think about yourself trying to have some fun (e.g., depression, money, location, creativity)? _____

_____

_____

4. Do you have any hang-ups about having fun, such as feeling guilty? _____

_____

_____

5. When you think of people you enjoy or have fun with, who comes to mind and why do you think you enjoy them? What makes them fun? _____

_____

_____

6. If you have thoughts such as "Fun is frivolous," why do you think you hold that belief? _____

_____

_____

7. In what small ways do you think you can integrate some fun into your life?

_____

_____

_____

8. What do you think it would take for you to become a little more fun, or to make your life more fun? _____

_____

_____

Fun and enjoyable things don't have to be elaborate or expensive. Here are some that you can do right away:

- Walk through a park
- Window-shopping
- People watching at an airport or mall
- Visit a zoo
- Rent your favorite movie
- Plant a flower or a tree
- Start a garden
- Rearrange the furniture in your home
- Look at photo albums
- Read books and magazines at the library or local bookstores

- Go to a park and lay out a blanket with a friend or a book
- Watch a sunset or sunrise
- Watch kids' shows or cartoons on TV
- Go to a free workshop or lecture
- Sign up to speak at a workshop or lecture at your local library or bookstore
- Go to open microphone poetry readings or musical performances
- Visit art galleries
- Get a facial at a department store
- Try cooking a new dish
- Adopt a pet from your local humane society
- Other: _____

Daily Positive Experiences

Go out of your way to create positive experiences in your daily life. Here are some simple pleasures you might consider:

- Take long, hot, luxurious showers or baths
- Have cocoa with whipped cream
- Walk through a local park or neighborhood
- Read
- Watch a TV sitcom
- Try samples at a deli
- Go to local festivals
- Go to local free live music or arts events
- Play a soothing or upbeat CD
- Watch your favorite TV show
- Tell someone that you love them
- Get your hair cut, styled, or highlighted
- Get a manicure or pedicure
- Take a nap
- Walk along a river or creek, or the seashore

- Get a back rub

- Sleep in one day this week

- Get a massage

- Get your favorite food, then eat it slowly and mindfully, savoring every bite

- Sit in a park while reading a book

- Write funny poems

- Slowly savor your favorite latte or herbal tea

- Sit for a while longer than usual in your favorite café or bookstore

- Other: _____

  _____

  _____

From my therapy experience, I know that for some people having fun is actually one of the hardest things they can do. But fun is a powerful aid if you want to regulate your emotions. It can keep you busy, give you happy memories, and increase your endorphins. Best of all, it's usually free.

For one week, practice doing one thing per day that you find to be pleasurable. These events don't have to be opulent or complicated. Most of the ones on the list above are very simple. Use the following worksheet to record your first solid week of the practice of pleasure. Next to the corresponding day, write the pleasure that you practiced. For example, you might write, "Got massage," or "Walked through park." In the box next to the pleasure, briefly describe how that felt. For example, you might write, "Relieved," "Cheerful," maybe even "Guilty"—whatever the case happened to be. In the obstacles column, write what seems to get in the way of your atttempts to increase positive events. For example, "Had argument with spouse."

A Week of Pleasures

Day	Pleasure	How I Felt	Obstacles?
Mon			
Tue			
Wed			
Thu			
Fri			
Sat			
Sun			

Long-Term Lifestyle Changes

Over the longer term, incorporating large and small changes in your life can yield a continuous stream of pleasure or benefit. Some of these will make you feel better. Others will help you avoid hassles that may have brought too much emotion in the past. None are esoteric or mysterious. All are gifts that keep on giving.

- Learn a new sport

- Travel

- Learn a new language

- Adopt a stance of gratitude

- Pray or meditate more often

- Write letters to friends and family

- Read more books

- Eat more vegetables

- Call your relatives more often

- Take up dance lessons

- Learn photography

- Stop collecting junk

- Pay bills on time

- Stretch more often

- Organize old pictures into albums or boxes

- File papers, forms, and bank statements

- Ask for help more often

- Say no more often

- Delegate more tasks

- Reduce credit card debt

- Drink more water

- Other: _____

_____

_____

Staying Mindful of the Positive

Sometimes life seems hectic and hateful because you lose sight of what is positive and exciting. Just when you're having a good time, you start worrying about when the good time will end. What makes this worse is that it's circular. Negative expectations will fulfill themselves by triggering negative emotions or by choking off positive ones. They can become a template through which you look at life, causing you to interpret positive events as more negative than they are. Staying mindful to the positive requires that you practice your mindfulness skills. Practice simply experiencing a positive situation as a positive situation, letting go of worry thoughts or thoughts about when the good time will end.

Here are some guidelines to staying mindful to positive emotions:

- Notice the positive emotion as it happens

- Don't cling to the positive emotion

- Don't push it away

- Let go of worry thoughts

- Let go of thoughts about when the positive event or feeling will end

- Stay present with what you feel

- Don't let fear or worry get in the way

Mindfulness to the Positive Exercises

The following are exercises you should follow exactly at first, then start varying a little after you attain a degree of mastery. And of course you can make substitutions if you need to. Don't drink hot coffee or tea? Try orange juice. The details are less important than your overall goal, which is a life more awake and alive to each moment as it happens. Don't let the positive simply pass you by, and don't let your worry thoughts rob you of living as fully as you can these beautiful and pleasant moments. Don't avoid the positive.

Drinking Your Favorite Hot Drink

If you buy your drink a restaurant or café, decide ahead of time that you will sit in the café for a while, taking your time. Hold your hot drink in your hands. Feel the warmth of the drink radiating through your cup or mug. Notice how your hands and skin respond to that warmth. Slowly lift the drink to your nose. Slowly and deliberately take in the smell of the drink. Be attentive to the aroma filtering through your nostrils. Let your sense of smell be alive to the aroma. Take your first sip very slowly and deliberately. Let the drink slowly wash through your mouth and over your tongue. Try to notice the flavor or mixture of flavors. Describe them to yourself. Is it bitter? Sour? Sweet? Milky?

As you continue this attentiveness to your drink be alert to any worry thoughts, thoughts of work, school, church, and home. Let these thoughts come and go. Don't hold on to them. Simply notice these outside thoughts, let them go and gently bring your awareness back to your drink. Right now, your drink is all that this moment is about. As distractions come and go, use your breath to become centered again at this precise moment of practice, neither going to the future, even if it's only a few minutes away, nor the past, even if it was a short while ago. Stay in this moment with this experience as long as you can. As you finish your drink you can allow yourself to return to your work, reading, or people watching.

Listening to Your Favorite Music

Pick out your favorite piece of music. As you play it, close your eyes and clear your mind of anything else. Give your full attention to everything about the music, being mindful of the beat, harmonies, and effects. Try to notice and describe to yourself as many instruments as you possibly can. Don't do anything else, just listen to the music, let yourself get swept away with the sounds, become one with the music. If you notice concerns for later in the day coming to your mind, simply notice these thoughts, labeling them as just that, then let them go. Gently bring your mind back to the sounds. Be aware of your pleasure triggered by the music. Listen to a whole set of music. If you have only time for one song, then give it your full attention, all of yourself to being present with that music, letting go of any worry thoughts or associations with music. Don't think about when the song or songs will end.

Getting a Massage

Schedule a professional massage for yourself. When you go, let yourself fully experience your muscles relaxing under the caring hands of your massage therapist. Notice the smell of the oils, or the incense or aromas in the room. Allow yourself to feel the pleasure of touch or the joy of being nurtured. If you notice your thoughts drifting to judgments about this activity, notice them, let them go, and gently come back to simply experiencing the massage. If you find yourself drifting away from the moment, don't judge yourself, but gently guide your awareness and attention back to where you are at this moment. Let yourself live in the moment. Don't miss out on the present by being pulled to the past or the future. Don't think about work. If you feel guilty for being self-indulgent, simply notice and label your guilt and then let it go. In this moment your mission and purpose are to fully experience the massage.

Reading a Favorite Book

Choose a book that you love to read. It can be fiction, nonfiction, poetry, religious literature, whatever. Let yourself become engrossed in what you read. When you read, simply read without letting your thoughts wander all over. If you notice that your thoughts are wandering, take a centering breath, and gently bring your mind back to reading. Allow yourself to become engrossed and lost in what you read, or try to memorize parts of what you read. Let the author take you where the story or literature goes. Don't judge what you read, simply participate in the act of reading. Read out loud if you can and if you think it will help your attention. Try this for periods of one hour, or several hours. You may have to start with five minutes. Whatever time you read, only read, that will be your purpose for the duration of that activity.

Walking through the Park

Find a park in your area that feels comfortable and pick a safe time to walk through it. If there isn't a park nearby, choose a local neighborhood where there are plenty of trees and as little traffic as possible. As you walk, notice the sights of the trees, flowers, houses, and people. Taking all of this in, let yourself feel the emotion of joy in response to beauty and peace. If there is sunshine, be mindful to that and the beauty inherent to the sun and the colors that it reflects. If it's sprinkling or raining, notice the beauty of the coolness and damp that brings forth life and nourishes living things. Do all that you can to abandon yourself to this moment, not letting work or worries pull you away. Don't be mindful to what is happening tomorrow. Tomorrow has enough trouble of its own. Simply be present in your walk. Feel your feet touching the ground and lifting, noticing your stride as you walk along at whatever pace is natural to you. Give yourself a good hour to thoroughly enjoy your walk.

Mindfulness to the Positive

Just like all the other skills that you're learning and practicing, do these over and over as often as you can until they become second nature. Use the following worksheet to record these and other pleasant events that you come up with on your own.

Describe your pleasant activity: _____

_____

_____

What positive emotions did you notice? _____

_____

_____

Describe how you clung to or pushed away any positive emotion(s): _____

_____

_____

Describe any worry thoughts and how you let go of them: _____

_____

_____

Describe how you did at letting go of thoughts about when the positive would end:

_____

_____

Describe how effective you were at staying present with your positive experience:

_____

_____

Describe how fear or worry got in the way, if they did: _____

_____

_____

As you increase your emotional resilience, you may find your emotions losing some of their power to knock you off your pins. In the next chapter, we'll explore a few techniques whereby you can actually change the character of strong emotions—defuse them, if you will. We'll discuss specific tactics—including what DBT calls *opposite to emotion*—to change strong emotions so they don't keep you from going to work or school, or facing the challenges of daily life.

CHAPTER 11

Changing Strong Emotions

You may remember that we said that when a specific emotion gets started, it fires a whole physiological system required for you to experience that emotion. That emotional set keeps re-firing over and over, in case you still need to be ready to take the action associated with that emotion.

If you get word that a very dear person died, you'll become sad. From the moment you begin to experience sadness you may experience other emotions, but you will be especially vulnerable to experiencing sadness or grief. Physiologically, your body loses energy and you may feel like avoiding company. But there are times when you need to go to work or school, or face an important challenge, and strong emotions can interfere with your effectiveness. If you need to give a presentation at work or school that absolutely can't be canceled, you'll have to change the emotion so that you can properly engage your audience or class.

Let's be clear about one thing: changing strong emotions doesn't mean invalidating them. It means redirecting them, putting them on hold, or taking their energy and making it useful. The idea is to take potentially destructive emotions and defuse them, so they don't threaten or interfere with your life.

Special Strategies for Strong Emotions

To change strong emotions, you first have identify them, of course. And to know what you feel, you have to go back to your mindfulness skills. You must be aware enough to identify what you're feeling and also to be aware of how strong emotion affects you so that you can know what you need to do to change it. In this section we'll review action urges and functions associated with specific emotions, and then give special attention to emotions that can spell trouble for many people. (Hint: one of the main culprits is love.)

Changing strong emotions involves four basic steps. Together, they help you become aware of your feelings, then take actions that slow or stop the feelings and their implications. The four steps are:

1. *Practice mindfulness to emotion (observe and describe)* so that you become aware of what you feel and experience, and then can know what to do.

2. *Change your body language and posture.* They're giving your brain feedback to keep firing the emotion that you want to change.

3. *Change your facial expression.* Like posture, it changes the feedback your brain gets in order to know what emotion it thinks you need.

4. *Engage in behaviors opposite to the emotion* that you're feeling so that you interrupt the emotion that is currently firing and re-firing. This means choosing behaviors that are incompatible with the emotion you're targeting for change.

Taking Action Opposite to the Emotion

Starting with step number four, let me say right away that action that is opposite to emotion *is not* always called for. There are times when your emotions match a given context or situation, and are appropriate. You will want to practice opposite action when your emotions are *too* strong, when you're being swept away by your emotions, and they get in the way rather than help.

Of course this is all very well in the abstract, but I know that putting it into practice can be tough. Suppose you're terrified of asking someone for a date. What would opposite action require you to do? Ask them for a date, of course. And if you're turned down, ask the next person out, and do this as often as you can. Are you afraid of speaking in public? Take a class on public speaking, fully participate in it, and plan to bravely give a talk when your turn comes. The trick is to "act as if." When you act as if you aren't angry, you'll eventually stop feeling anger. If you act as if you aren't sad, your sadness will lift.

For opposite action to be effective, you have to do it again and again, until your emotions change. It may take a while before you notice any change, so don't give up right away. You have to really let go of judgments about yourself and your situation—even your practice of opposite emotion. You must throw yourself completely into opposite action, doing all that you can to engage your whole being and your whole self into doing, thinking, and eventually feeling differently. Allow yourself to feel differently, letting go of too much anger, or too much sadness, or too much worry. Participate with awareness to your every move, and focus on effective outcomes.

Opposite to Anger

Intense anger can get in the way of your work. You may feel tense and be distracted by thoughts related to what or who triggered your anger. Look at the following list and check all that apply to you when you're too angry, and add your own responses in the blanks that follow.

When I'm feeling very angry I tend to:

☐ Drive fast or aggressively

☐ Glare at people

☐ Be aggressive toward other people

☐ Displace my angry feelings on the wrong people

☐ Say things I might regret

☐ Find people avoiding me

☐ Feel isolated

☐ Push, shove, or punch somebody

☐ Have an upset stomach or lose my appetite

☐ Feel stressed or wired

☐ Experience heart trouble or high blood pressure

☐ Lose sleep

☐ Relapse with addiction (if in recovery)

☐ Throw or break things

☐ Say something impulsive or that I regret later

☐ Interfere with learning or listening

☐ Interfere with job performance

☐ Dwell on wrongs or revenge fantasies

☐ Other: _____

_____

_____

To change your anger, take these four steps:

1. Practice mindfulness to anger (observe and describe)

- I notice that a wave of anger is washing over me
- I notice that my teeth are tightly clenched

- I observe tension in my upper shoulders
- I notice the urge to shout/push/scream/swear/throw, etc.
- I observe the thought, "I hate so-and-so!"
- I observe the thought, "Life/job/school is unfair!"
- Other: _____

_____

_____

2. Change body language and posture

- Take three deep centering breaths
- If your hands are balled into fists, loosen and open them
- Change an aggressive stance to a friendly and inviting one
- Put your hands in your pockets

3. Change facial expression

- Adopt a half smile (not a smirk)
- Take an expression that you think communicates serenity
- Make a face of compassion
- Use your face to communicate interest in others
- Use your face to communicate gentleness
- Other: _____

_____

_____

4. Engage in behaviors that are opposite to the anger you're feeling

- Tell someone how you care about them
- Tell someone, "I love you"
- Stare at a tree
- Go get a massage
- Gently avoid the person you are angry with
- Be extra careful to gently pick up and set down items
- Slowly and mindfully drink a cold glass of water
- Hug someone
- Pray for your enemies

- Think about how life might be hard for the person you're angry with

- Pay a compliment to the person you're upset with

- Say out loud to yourself, "I can handle this situation"

- If you're driving, be extra cautious, and drive more slowly than usual

- Take five minutes to stretch muscles in your upper and lower body

- Think about things that are inconsistent with anger, such as happy times, beautiful places, successes

- Listen to soothing music and love songs

- Other: _____

_____

_____

Opposite to Fear

Left unchecked, intense fear can play havoc with your quality of life. It can interfere with your productivity, relationships, personal development, travel, and many other things. Extreme cases of fear include panic attacks and agoraphobia, a disorder in which people become so fearful they can hardly bear to go outside. Check the items on the following list that apply.

When I'm feeling very frightened, I tend to:

- ☐ Get an upset stomach

- ☐ Miss parties, classes, or work

- ☐ Avoid travel

- ☐ Avoid going outdoors

- ☐ Not start or finish projects

- ☐ Second-guess myself

- ☐ Feel paranoia or suspicion

- ☐ Avoid new and interesting experiences

- ☐ Avoid new and interesting people, and dating

- ☐ Avoid public performances

- ☐ Lose my appetite

- ☐ Lose sleep

- ☐ Have clouded thoughts

- ☐ Have racing thoughts ("monkey mind")

☐ Not get things done now because I'm worrying about the future

☐ Not look for new work that interests me

☐ Avoid going to school

☐ Other: _____

_____

_____

To change your fear, take these four steps:

1. Practice mindfulness to fear (observe and describe)

- I notice fear has just fallen on me

- I observe that my thoughts are numerous and busy

- I notice I feel butterflies in my stomach

- I observe that I'm avoiding a person or situation

- I feel a strong urge to flee

- I notice the thought, "I can't handle this situation" has entered my mind

- I notice that I have thoughts that others will know how nervous I am

- I notice that my body is shaking or tense

- Other: _____

_____

_____

2. Change body language and posture

- Stand upright

- Make appropriate eye contact with others

- Sit comfortably

- Look up at the sky for a while

- Keep your head high

- Stand with confidence

- Walk with confidence

- Sit upright in your chair with hands gently folded

- Let your hands lie still on your desktop or tabletop, not tapping them

- Sit still without tapping your feet

- Other: _____

_____

_____

3. Change facial expression

- Try to adopt a "serious" facial expression

- Try to imitate a face of confidence

- Adopt a half smile

- Adopt a serene facial expression

- Try to look at others with an expression of interest

- Other: _____

_____

_____

4. Engage in behaviors that are opposite to the fear you're feeling

- Approach the thing or person you fear.

- If you fear going to school, go to school.

- If you fear traveling, take opportunities to go on short trips to nearby towns or sites.

- If you fear asking some one out, do so. If you're turned down, ask the next person out, and then the next.

- Attend parties you're invited to. Once you're there, greet people, introduce yourself, get into it.

- If you're anxious about looking for a new job, schedule several appointments, even at job sites you don't necessarily want to work at.

- Throw your whole self into your practice, get into it.

- Other: _____

_____

_____

Opposite to Sadness or Grief

Have you ever heard the expression, "Don't build your house at the cemetery"? I like the saying because it acknowledges that cemeteries are real. They are places for mourning and memorializing. Cemeteries validate our losses. But building your house there means making yourself live in misery when you don't have to. If you live at the cemetery you will miss out on the rest of your life, and the wonderful experiences that only happen outside the cemetery. Practice these skills if your sadness or grief goes on too long or is too strong. Look at this checklist of some of the problems that too much sadness can lead to.

When I'm feeling very sad, I tend to:

☐ Feel depressed and apathetic

☐ Lose time dwelling on the thing or person I lost

☐ Find my relationships suffer because I'm dwelling on my loss

☐ Lose my appetite

☐ Sleep too much or not enough

☐ Think I'll never love again

☐ Resent those who seem happy

☐ Contemplate suicide

☐ Have lowered immunity to sicknesses

☐ Reject others' attempts to get to know me

☐ Am forgetful

☐ Feel bitter

☐ Act mean toward other people

☐ Other: _____

_____

_____

To change your sadness, take these four steps:

1. Practice mindfulness to sadness

- I observe a veil of sadness falling over me

- I notice my energy draining

- I observe grief rising inside me

- I feel tears welling up in my eyes

2. Change body language and posture

- Lift head up

- Sit up straight

- Walk upright

- Watch comedies on TV

- Listen to uplifting music

3. Change facial expression

- Wear a half smile

- Smile at other people

- Adopt a face of confidence

- Make eye contact with others at work, school, or home

4. Engage in behaviors that are opposite to the sadness you're feeling

- Approach activities that you must do rather than avoid

- Go to work, school, or religious services

- Exercise

- Eat meals

- Sing hymns, fight songs, or hum triumphant tunes

- Maintain your personal hygiene

- Dress up

- Go for walks

- Spend time at the library or bookstores

When Good Emotions Go Bad

As we have seen, some emotions that we usually think of as negative can have positive and adaptive functions. Anger, for example, can help energize you to overcome obstacles. Conversely, emotions that feel good can sometimes become problematic.

Becoming too interested in a subject or person can become an obsession or addiction, and a detriment to your work or relationships. If you become completely lost in research on a topic you can ignore your friends or family; months or years down the road, you'll wonder why you aren't intimate with them. Even work or study that requires a lot of time, such as pursuing a degree or graduate education, can become too involved and threaten relationships outside your work or study circles.

Do you have something like a new computer that you're learning how to use, or are tinkering with? Have you gotten so interested the computer that when friends come over to visit you and your family, you slip off to play with your toy? Legitimate interests can require unusual amounts of time, but don't necessarily require that you sacrifice all intimacy with your loved ones. Sometimes interests may be effective tools for avoidance of relationships, and you can mask your obsessions behind a facade of importance or legitimacy.

If I had to name one positive emotion with the potential to cause more trouble than all the others combined, it would have to be love and attraction—that is, when you're attracted to someone who is *not* your partner or spouse.

Love and Attraction

As with any emotion, feeling attraction or even romantic love toward a person other than your spouse or partner isn't unusual or bad; it's part of being alive. But what you do with that emotion—what you make of it and how you act on it—is what makes the difference as to whether or not it will be a problem.

If you let your attraction or love feelings pull you into private liaisons, you might begin a pattern of behavior that could jeopardize your current relationship and everything you have put into building it. Affairs don't usually start with bad intentions. Most people say they happen as a matter of "falling in love" with a person other than the committed partner. Intrigue, attraction, and interest combine to sweep you into a new relationship that will threaten your current one.

Even where there isn't another relationship to worry about, there are a host of other dangers of feeling love that isn't balanced with your logic and wisdom. They include sexually transmitted diseases, unwanted or unexpected pregnancy, and the heartbreak that follows when you realize the other person didn't share your depth of feeling or crave intimacy as much as they may have craved sexual release. Sometimes intense love feelings and attraction lead people into relationships that are violent or expose them to crime or exploitation.

All of this isn't to say don't trust your love or your attraction, but experience them as emotions, keep your wisdom sharp, and keep an eye on your personal values, not sacrificing them to impulsiveness.

Is Love Becoming a Problem?

If new love emotions become a threat to an existing relationship, here are some questions you might ask yourself:

- What do I want in the long run?

- What behaviors would threaten the life and health of my current relationship?

- What behaviors for this situation most closely match my moral values?

- Is there something I need from my spouse or partner that I haven't expressed?

- How can I turn the energy of this attraction toward my current relationship?

- What would I actually gain from pursuing this new person?

Here are some of signs that you're becoming emotionally overinvolved with that other person:

- Taking walks, lunches, or coffees alone with the other person

- Telling the other person about your own relationship problems

- The other person tells you about their relationship problems

- You eagerly look forward to seeing that person

- You anticipate spending time alone with that person

- You keep your discussions and meetings with the other person a secret from your spouse or partner

- You feel sexually charged around that person

- You exchange gifts without telling your spouse or partner

- You begin comparing your spouse or partner to the other person

To change your love and attraction, take these four steps:

1. Practice mindfulness to love and attraction

- I observe a feeling of attraction toward so-and-so

- I notice that I feel intensely excited when I am with that person

- I notice feelings of arousal when we are alone

- I notice the emotion of love

- I observe wanting to give love to this person

- I notice that I think about sex with this person

- I feel a warmth around me when I am with that person

2. Change body language, posture, and location

- Don't stand close to the person

- Don't spend time alone with the person that you're strongly attracted to

- Don't dress for that person or wear cologne or perfume you think they would like

- Don't maintain a doting or lingering gaze

- Avoid inappropriate hugging, hand-holding, rubbing, or caressing

3. Change facial expression

- Adopt a platonic face, whatever you think that looks like when talking with other platonic friends

- Don't make direct eye contact for very long

- Adopt half smiling

4. Engage in behaviors that are opposite to the love and attraction you're feeling

- Think of this person as your brother or sister

- Incorporate your spouse or partner into your discussions with the other person, refer to "my wife," or "my husband," or use their name, especially when you have the urge to not bring them up or keep them a secret

- Avoid dressing in a way that you think that person would find attractive or provocative

- Tell your spouse or partner about your interactions with this person, especially when you notice that you'd rather keep them a secret

- Avoid being alone with this person, especially when you notice that you strongly desire it

- Avoid intimate conversation with that person

- Don't ask them out on a date

- Invite the other person to parties or situations where they meet your partner, so your partner becomes a living reality for both of you

- Keep pictures of your spouse or partner on your desk or in your workspace

- Tell your spouse or partner about your attraction or infatuation

- Tell a good friend about your infatuation with this person

- Respectfully decline any advances from this person

- Gently avoid the person altogether, if need be

- Avoid private meetings, lunches, or coffees with the attractive person

- When you talk to the other person mention the positive qualities of your spouse or partner

- If you have a gripe about your spouse or partner, tell it to your dog, your friend, clergyperson, or therapist—but not the person you're attracted to

- Acknowledge your emotions, and thereby recognize that you're alive

- Observe and describe physiological reactions (arousal, racing heart, changes in breathing)

- Observe and describe urges related to your attraction or love emotion

- Acknowledge the qualities that attract you to this person (physical, intellectual, shared interest)

- Validate your experience, telling yourself that this is normal

Turning Knowledge into Skills

The last part of this book focuses on taking everything we've learned so far and turning it into practical skills for daily living. Chapter 12 deals generally with relationship skills, including dealing with difficult people. Chapter 13 zeroes in on ways to deal with those people we love—and occasionally hate—our intimate friends, spouses, and partners. Finally, in chapter 14, you'll learn specific techniques for handling crises and soothing yourself that will help you skillfully cope with distress and anxiety.

PART IV

Leading an Emotionally Skillful Life

CHAPTER 12

Relationship Skills

Emotions connect to you to other people and to the world around you, and primary adaptive emotions can facilitate relationships with other people. "Emotion is thus a relational experience connecting the individual and the environment; people experience emotion in relation to people or objects in the world that they are angry at, sad about, or afraid of" (Greenberg and Johnson, 1988).

But sometimes when you need to communicate to others, your emotion may be too strong or too weak. Or there's a mismatch between your facial expressions and what you're saying to get your message across. In this chapter and the next, we're going to focus on developing effective ways of communicating emotion to the people around us. In this chapter, we'll deal with relationship skills in general. In chapter 13, we'll focus on our intimate relationships. In both, we'll be talking about what DBT therapists formally call *InterPersonal Effectiveness* (IPE) skills.

Interpersonal Effectiveness Skills

In DBT, interpersonal effectiveness skills include how to ask for what you need, how to tell others "no," and how to cope with conflicts you may face with all kinds of people (family, friends, coworkers, teachers, etc.). The skills may sound quite commonsensical, but they can be hard to implement.

If you need to let someone know that you're angry with them, pouting or speaking softly won't express the degree of your anger very effectively. The other person might think you are slightly annoyed and not "get" that you're really quite mad. IPE is all about getting that emotion across in a way that is clear and effective.

In which of these settings and situations might you benefit from having IPE skills?

- Home

- Work

- School

- Shopping

- Dining out

- Being pulled over for a speeding ticket

- Asking your employer for a raise

- Family reunion

- Legal proceedings

- Asking someone out on a date

- Negotiating with friends what movie you want to see

- Getting someone to acknowledge a wrong

- Having someone tell you you're wrong

- Public speaking

- Driving

- Holiday get-together

- Play groups and dates

- Taking child to school for first time

- Parent-teacher conferences

Rating Your Current IPE

Before looking at your current IPE skill set, let's look at your foundations for interpersonal effectiveness.

How did your parents model reciprocity for you? _____

_____

_____

_____

How did your family of origin respond to your needs when you made requests or communicated a need? _____

_____

_____

_____

Were you encouraged to express your needs when you were growing up? If so, how? If not, why do you think this is the case? _____

_____

_____

_____

During your childhood how did you get others to take your problems, needs, or feelings seriously? _____

_____

_____

_____

How do you get others to take your problems, needs, and feelings seriously these days?

_____

_____

_____

How do your emotions sometimes get in the way of expressing your needs?

_____

_____

_____

Do you think you are skilled at accepting it when you're told no, or tolerating negative answers to requests? Explain your answer: _____

_____

_____

_____

If you are better with interpersonal effectiveness than you used to be, to what do you attribute that improvement? _____

_____

_____

_____

Does your spouse or partner seem to take you seriously when you express your needs or feelings? How do you know? _____

_____

_____

_____

How do you show your friends or family that you take their needs and feelings seriously? _____

_____

_____

_____

Your Personal IPE Inventory

Let's start by seeing how aware you are of your interpersonal resources and skills. Look at the following statements to get a sense of what you believe about your current level of skillfulness. Then take a moment to reflect on why you think you have or lack the resource or skill.

- I'm very skilled at asking for what I want

- I have people in my life whom I can ask for help

- I'm a "yes-man" or "yes-woman"

- I don't know how to ask for help

- When people say no it means they dislike me

- I have trouble saying no to requests

- I say yes to so much that I can't do anything

- Other people really aren't interested in helping me

- I rarely do favors for friends and family

- When someone tells me no once, it means they won't ever say yes

- When I want to say no I make up excuses to avoid having to say no

- I can tolerate and accept it when people say no to my requests

- I am deeply hurt when others say no to me

- I get upset thinking about asking for help from others

Now, for each statement on the list that you agree with, try to think of at least three specific examples or situations that support the way you feel. If you find that hard to do, even for statements that you strongly feel are true, ask yourself: What does that tell you about your belief?

Applying Interpersonal Effectiveness Skills

One of the most common situations in a relationship between people happens when one wants or needs something from the other. It's also one of the thorniest. There are a number of factors you need to consider when you ask others for help or favors, and when you refuse others' requests (which is often harder). How hard do you push to get what you want? How hard do you resist when you must say no? What are the unspoken elements in any negotiation, and what weight should you give them?

Applying IPE involves carefully weighing a number of critical interpersonal elements that are involved when you make a request or when someone makes a request of you. These elements are priorities, capability, timing, homework, authority, rights, reciprocity, long-term versus short-term problems, and respect.

In this tabulation, I have listed the questions you should ask yourself under each element. With time, those will become second nature, and your analysis of a situation will become faster and smoother.

Priorities

- Are my objectives very important?

- Is the relationship fragile, injured, or tenuous?

- Is my self-respect on the line?

- Will my self-respect be damaged if I say no to a request?

Capability

- Is the other person able to give me what I want?

- Do I have what the other person wants?

Timing

- Is the other person in the mood to listen?

- Is this a time when the other person is likely to say yes to my request?

- Is this a bad time for me to say no?

Homework

- Do I know enough about this situation or person of whom I'm making the request?

- Do I have all the information I need about this request?

- Am I clear about what I want?

- Is the other person's request clear?

- Do I know what I'm saying yes to, or committing to?

Authority

- Does the person making the request have authority over me?

- Do I have authority over the person I'm asking to do something?

Rights

- Would saying yes to the request violate my rights in any way?

- Would saying no to the request violate that person's rights?

Reciprocity

- Have I done as much for this person as I am asking them to do for me?

- Has the other person done as much for me as they are asking of me?

Long-Term versus Short-Term

- Will giving up on my request now result in long-term problems later?

- Will saying to no to the other person's request lead to long-term problems?

Respect

- Do I usually do things for myself?

- Do I avoid appearing helpless?

- Will saying no make me feed bad about myself?

If the approach seems obvious to you, congratulations. You already have a well-honed grasp of the subtleties of dealing with requests and other people. But for most of us, exchanges within even familiar relationships can sometimes be mysterious. And for many people, almost every aspect of a negotiation—having to ask for help, being pressured to say yes, forcing yourself to say no—is stressful. Coolly analyzing the elements of an exchange can help us make that all-important choice between yes and no.

Mindfulness to Personal Interactions

If you apply the analytical IPE skills described above, you will make smarter choices. And if you add the mindfulness skills you've learned, you'll make wiser ones.

Observe and describe what is going on in the situation. Describe to yourself what the other person is actually saying and actually doing. Just put words on what is happening without editorializing or letting your mind wander to assumptions or what you think you know about the situation or the other person's motives. For example, "I notice that Barb is asking me to put the toilet seat lid down . . . I notice I'm feeling anxious . . . I notice the thought, 'I wish this wasn't an issue.'" That's vastly different than, "That nag Barb, all she does is complain about that dang toilet lid!"

Take a nonjudgmental stance. Be attentive to your judgments and assumptions about the other person or their motives and then let go of them. Be intentionally compassionate toward the other person(s) and toward yourself as you work for an effective outcome. Remember that judgments are often conditioned reactions that don't always accurately reflect the situation and sometimes cause you emotional suffering. Don't evaluate this situation as you work it out, see it, and accept it.

Stay present. Don't leave the discussion abruptly or without warning. Don't let your mind wander to worry thoughts about how this will turn out awfully for you. Become so engaged with this situation and the other person(s) that you are no longer self-conscious. Don't make excuses to get out of the discussion or situation, dissociate, or tune out. Be where you are, with your full attention and intention.

Stay willing. Be willing and open to stay in the discussion, even if it's difficult. With respect to others allow yourself to feel your connection to them.

Checking Out Assumptions: Jenny

In our couples therapy sessions, Jenny often went on the attack in session, while John would sit in silence, taking it in, with a mildly pained expression on his face. Jenny would rattle off a litany of complaints about John in session and then finish for a moment by saying, "Do you see what I have to live with? See how passive he is? He just doesn't care. He never has."

Eventually, we established that there was a pattern in their relationship of Jenny being quite forceful in her opinion which came across too strongly for John, so rather than risk further escalation he would retreat into himself. He expressed that it didn't matter what he said or did, she was never happy with it because she treated his efforts to be involved at home as substandard.

Jenny was willing to practice checking out her assumptions about John's behavior. For instance, when he wouldn't offer his opinion she assumed that he didn't want to talk. As it turned out, she wasn't waiting for his reply. She started talking again before he could respond. John simply didn't know how to get a word in with Jenny talking over him, and he didn't want to escalate her emotions, nor his. This was news to Jenny. Every time Jenny told John why he was doing something (e.g., "You don't talk because you don't care"), she had to ask John to confirm or deny whether her assumption about his motives were correct. Almost always she was wrong. And she began to see how her assumptions affected her emotional responses to John.

We all worked together to balance having Jenny wait for responses from John, and letting go of old and incorrect assumptions. And we worked with John to be more responsive in a way that Jenny could appreciate. They worked at moving toward the middle, closer to one another, and with a new skill of checking out their mutual assumptions about one another, thus having fewer obstacles to overcome.

People You Are Especially Sensitive To

In everybody's life, there is at least one person that we have a relationship with that is thorny, tender, easily ruffled, or in some other way sensitive. Some of us have several or many such people in our lives. Try making a list of the elements of such a relationship. Make a copy of the worksheet for each person on your list.

Especially Difficult People

Person's name: _____

Describe your relationship to this person: _____

_____

_____

Describe the quality of this relationship: _____

_____

_____

Why do you think you are especially sensitive to this relationship? _____

_____

_____

Describe how you would like to improve this relationship: _____

_____

_____

List potential obstacles to improving how you relate with this person: _____

_____

_____

Dealing with Difficult People

Now refine your list to focus on people you're not only sensitive to, but people who you find especially difficult to be around, or *aversive*. Maybe they act caustic, rude, or shaming toward you and others. Around them you find yourself becoming very nervous, resentful, or fearful. Sometimes these people may be family members that you have to see at family functions. Or they may be coworkers that you can't completely avoid at a job. In either case, the effect of being around them is to sometimes leave you feeling absolutely miserable.

If you find yourself in such a setting, consider the following practices to help you change your emotional responses so your experiences become more bearable.

When I use the word aversive in reference to the other person, I mean that the other person has become someone that you would greatly like to avoid. You may even find yourself judging them as repulsive, repugnant, or disgusting. You may find that you hate them, and feel they are worthy of your contempt. As you begin the work of changing your emotions toward this other person, however, try to avoid those thoughts. The idea here is to move away from unnecessary emotional suffering and toward effectiveness so that you don't carry the burden of your intense negative emotions. The goal is to reduce your emotional suffering. Also keep in mind that the goal isn't to change that other person. Instead, you're working at changing yourself.

For the following exercise, list up to five people you find extremely difficult and aversive. Choose people you have regular contact with: daily, weekly, or at least monthly. Don't pick people you only see once a year (although I hope you'll extend your practice to your interactions with them, too). You need regular practice, so that's why I urge you to target situations in which you are engaged with these difficult people. Start with a difficult-person inventory to build awareness to who it is you consider difficult and why they are difficult to you.

Five Difficult People: An Inventory

1. Name: _____

Level of difficulty (0-5): _____

Context of interaction: _____

Describe how you feel around this person: _____

_____

Describe your judgments about this person: _____

_____

Describe how you currently handle being around this person: _____

_____

2. Name: _____

Level of difficulty (0-5): _____

Context of interaction: _____

Describe how you feel around this person: _____

_____

Describe your judgments about this person: _____

_____

Describe how you currently handle being around this person: _____

_____

3. Name: _____

Level of difficulty (0-5): _____

Context of interaction: _____

Describe how you feel around this person: _____

_____

Describe your judgments about this person: _____

_____

Describe how you currently handle being around this person: _____

_____

4. Name: _____

Level of difficulty (0-5): _____

Context of interaction: _____

Describe how you feel around this person: _____

_____

Describe your judgments about this person: _____

_____

Describe how you currently handle being around this person: _____

_____

5. Name: _____

Level of difficulty (0-5): _____

Context of interaction: _____

Describe how you feel around this person: _____

_____

Describe your judgments about this person: _____

_____

Describe how you currently handle being around this person: _____

_____

Now that you have assessed your "top five," as it were, it's time for you to commit yourself to engaging in facing these difficult persons in a new and skillful manner.

Be prepared for potential obstacles, including intense painful emotions, worry thoughts, or thoughts about your inability to change or handle these situations. You'll need to prepare yourself before facing the difficult person, and once you face them you must resolve to follow through with your new skills practice, and do it in the heat of the moment. This is where real change takes place. Also, don't expect that you'll change the way you react to these people overnight. You'll have to engage them over and over again. Change may come slowly, but if you stick with it, you'll experience change—and I believe you'll be quite excited about it.

One more caveat. The change won't be from fearing or loathing a person to enjoying their presence. If that comes, so much the better. But for starters keep your sights on the primary goal, which is reducing the degree of negative emotion you'll feel.

Using Exposure Therapy Methods

What you are about to embark on is similar to techniques used in *exposure therapy*, where you face objects or situations that you typically fear or avoid—heights, snakes, cats, flying—until your anxiety about facing them is reduced or gone. In your case, this happens by virtue of being exposed to the difficult person and engaging in breathing and opposite action. As you face your fears again and again, you'll become less impaired by them. (By the way, if you find any of this hard, that's natural. If it were easy, we would have done it long ago.)

Here are some exposure strategies and how to use them:

Observe and describe. Observe and describe the other person's behaviors, simply stating what you actually see. Let go of your assumptions or what you think you know about this person and their motives; just stick to the facts. For example, "I observe that this person is speaking loudly" and "I notice this person uses a curt tone of voice." You can also use your observe and describe skills to become aware of your own thoughts. Simply notice them, without holding on to them or trying to push them away. "I notice that I have the thought 'I wish I didn't have to work with this person'" or "I observe the judgment that I wish this person would die." Know what your thoughts are as you have them, and don't judge yourself for having judgments. Just observe them as they arise.

Mindfulness to emotion. Be aware to what you are feeling—fear, anger, shame, whatever. Don't judge your emotions, but label them descriptively. Be aware of each emotion, just noticing experiencing it, and letting go of thoughts such as, "I can't stand this" or "I'm a basket case."

Opposite action. Actively engage the person. Instead of avoiding them, go out of your way to speak to them and do so with confidence and opposite to the emotion that you're feeling at that time. If you're angry, approach the person with gentleness and a half smile; ask them about their family or just how they are. If you absolutely have to get away because you have pushed past your current limits, avoid the person gently and deliberately, knowing that you are avoiding them because you choose to, and not out of mindless impulsivity.

Breathing. Remember to take centering breaths as you notice your emotions getting stronger. Breathing helps to center you and triggers a physiological relaxation response that will help you to more effectively endure the situation you are in, and even if it becomes hard, it won't remain impossible. Over time your body and brain will begin to make new associations with being in proximity to the difficult person. Breathing is how you get hold of your mind and cooperate with your emotions.

Nonjudgmental stance. Let go of your judgments about the difficult person. They ultimately only hurt you and don't change you or the person. Try looking at the person with new eyes, and see how you feel. Practice observing and describing their appearance. Do this factually, noting their size and eye and hair color. Stick to the facts and see if you can have a new view of that person.

Make a copy of the following worksheet for each difficult person in your life, and record your interactions. Make a note to reread the sheets in a few days or weeks. See any change?

Dealing with Difficult People

1. Name of difficult person: _____

Level of difficulty (0-5): ____

Predicted level of difficulty (0-100): ____

Skills you plan to use:

- Observe and describe

- Mindfulness to emotion

- Opposite action (actively engage person)

- Breathing

- Nonjudgmental stance toward difficult person

- Assertiveness

- Act out of self-respect

- Distress tolerance

Context of interaction: _____

Describe the situation: _____

_____

_____

Describe emotions that you felt around this person: _____

_____

_____

Describe skills used (opposite action, breathing, mindfulness): _____

_____

_____

_____

Rate actual difficulty of situation (0–100): ____

Rate your effectiveness: (0–100): ____

What you plan to do at your next interaction, and how you might improve your practice:

_____

_____

_____

As you interact with others, try to be aware of assumptions that you carry with you from your past, and your habits of thought that come with you into the present. Your assumptions may or may not reflect reality or truth, so simply practice being aware of what you are thinking.

The DEAR MAN GIVE FAST Mnemonic

Interpersonal effectiveness training has three major goals:

1. Objectives effectiveness: getting what you want

2. Relationship effectiveness: getting and keeping relationships

3. Self-respect effectiveness: how to feel good about yourself

In her skills training manual (1993b), Marsha Linehan offers a mnemonic device to remind people of the skills that address these three areas: DEAR MAN GIVE FAST. The first part, D-E-A-R M-A-N, lists factors involved in getting what you want. The second, G-I-V-E, focuses on the relationship. The third, F-A-S-T, deals with your self-respect.

DEAR MAN: Getting What I Want

We all need to communicate with others about what we want out of situations. Being emotionally connected to the environment means asking for things we need from friends, family, teachers, and employers. Sometimes you may not get what you want because very strong emotions get in the way; sometimes the environment doesn't respond to your best efforts. Even the most skillful people don't get what they want all the time, and there is a skill in accepting no in situations where you don't get what you want.

To work at getting what you want, use D-E-A-R M-A-N, which stands for the following:

Describe. Say words to the other person, describing what you want, and saying it as clearly as possible so that they know what you want. Be precise and descriptive, leaving no question in the other person's mind what it is that you want.

Express. Don't be afraid to be expressive. You're working at controlling your emotions, not being unemotional. Use facial expressions, gestures, and tone of voice that are appropriate to the content and importance of your request. Can you recall dull teachers or professors who spoke in a monotone and were unexpressive? Now compare them to those who waved their hands around a bit, and you'll think of reasons to be expressive. You want to make an impression on your own behalf.

Assert. Be assertive and matter-of-fact. Don't be aggressive or passive aggressive about your request, and don't threaten the other person or blow your stack.

Reinforce. Make sure that the other person knows why they should give you what you are asking for. If appropriate, tell them the positive outcomes for you, for them, and for your relationship. Use statements like, "It would mean the world to me if you . . ." or "I would be deeply grateful if you give me what I want," or (in extreme cases) "I'll wash your car for a month if you do this." Try to make the other person feel good about granting your request. But don't offer the other person something that you can't deliver. Be realistic and genuine.

Stay Mindful. Stay on track with your request. Keep your eye on the prize, and don't let distractions, worry thoughts, or the other person throw you off. If they attack you for making your request, ignore the attacks and keep pressing for what you want. If you let yourself get caught up in personal attacks or insults you'll be more vulnerable to overreacting. And if you engage in highly ineffective behaviors, that may sabotage the whole discussion or give the other person the excuse of not wanting to deal with an out-of-control "crazy person." Don't retaliate. Instead, practice opposite action, breathing, and radical acceptance.

Appear confident. Stand up straight and make good eye contact when making your request. Don't stammer or back off. Think of yourself as a confident and competent businessperson closing a sale, or as a successful negotiator. People will take you more seriously if you at least appear to take yourself seriously. Tie this in with your practice of self-validation, because your needs and wants are valid.

Negotiate. Without compromising your values, consider accepting a middle-ground solution that may be "good enough." Try to respect the other person's limits. Skillful negotiating may help you to get more of what you want in the future because you are able to demonstrate a respect for the limits of others, and you come across as reasonable, which can be an engaging quality that affords you future influence.

GIVE: Focusing on the Relationship

The G-I-V-E part of the mnemonic helps to strengthen the connection between you and the other person.

(Be) Gentle. Be gentle with the other person. Sometimes when emotions run high and feelings get hurt, people can turn nasty. This will only drive a wedge deeper between the two of you. Being gentle can change the whole tone of the interaction.

(Act) Interested. Truly listen to the other person, so they sense that you care about their perspective. Not only will you really get their position, but you'll get a more engaged and willing participant for the discussion.

Validate. Acknowledge what the other person expresses or demonstrates about their perspective, including their emotional experiences. You can do this by using statements such as, "I see that you are angry. I hear you saying that you're disappointed in my behavior."

(Use an) Easy manner. Be mellow and relaxed. Let of go of tension, anger, rage, and your judgments. As Linehan writes, this is the difference between the "soft sell" and the "hard sell" (1993b, 82). She suggests wheedling and schmoozing with others, including the use of humor, smiling, and soothing. This is much nicer and much more effective than being pushy or verbally aggressive.

FAST: Focusing on Your Self-Respect

Finally, bring your F-A-S-T skills to bear.

(Be) Fair. You have to give some to get some. Scratch others' backs as much as they scratch yours. You may damage your self-respect if you don't reciprocate. Others will notice how fair you are with them, so pay attention to this. When you're trying to solve problems, try to be fair to yourself and the other person.

(No) Apologies. Apologize when you are wrong, of course, but don't be overly apologetic. Don't apologize for taking up the other person's air, and try not to come across as pathetic and whiny. Nobody wants to hang out with whiny people. It could also damage your self-respect, because being overly apologetic can reinforce self-invalidation and old judgments about yourself, your effectiveness, and your worth as a person.

Stick to values. When appropriate, express your opinions on political, religious, and psychological issues. Don't keep quiet just to avoid being judged or sounding dumb. Let others know where you're coming from and don't change your mind on moral or value issues without a very good reason. Be careful not to confuse flexibility with a lack of integrity. You can hold opinions different from others and still respect and be respected in a spirit of true tolerance.

(Be) Truthful. Act according to your true level of skillfulness. Tell others what you need or want. If you distort the truth—by telling a white lie to spare someone's feelings, for example—make sure you know that you're doing it and do it mindfully and not reactively.

IPE Worksheet

Commit to one week of practice with these skills. But don't wait for major negotiations to use them. Try them out in small interpersonal transactions. Get friends or acquaintances to role-play with you. A little rehearsal will help you be better prepared to use the IPE skills when you need them in truly tough situations. Use the following worksheet to guide you in your practice.

On the days that you practice any of your IPE skills circle the skills in the corresponding column(s). In the last column rate the effectiveness of your skills practice (0 = no effectiveness, 1 = minimal effectiveness, 2 = mildly effective, 3 = moderately effective, 4 = very effective, 5 = extremely effective).

IPE Practice Diary (Example)				
DAY	**OBJECTIVES**	**RELATIONSHIP**	**SELF-RESPECT**	**EFFECTIVENESS (0-5)**
Mon	DEAR MAN	GIVE	FAST	2
Tue	DEAR MAN	GIVE	FAST	4
Wed	DEAR MAN	GIVE	FAST	0
Thu	DEAR MAN	GIVE	FAST	2
Fri	DEAR MAN	GIVE	FAST	5
Sat	DEAR MAN	GIVE	FAST	4
Sun	DEAR MAN	GIVE	FAST	2
NOTES: Need more practice on self-respect effectiveness				
Effectiveness rating: (0 = no effectiveness, 1 = minimal effectiveness, 2 = mildly effective, 3 = moderately effective, 4 = very effective, 5 = extremely effective)				

IPE Practice Diary

DAY	OBJECTIVES	RELATIONSHIP	SELF-RESPECT	EFFECTIVENESS (0-5)
Mon	DEAR MAN	GIVE	FAST	
Tue	DEAR MAN	GIVE	FAST	
Wed	DEAR MAN	GIVE	FAST	
Thu	DEAR MAN	GIVE	FAST	
Fri	DEAR MAN	GIVE	FAST	
Sat	DEAR MAN	GIVE	FAST	
Sun	DEAR MAN	GIVE	FAST	

NOTES:

Effectiveness rating: (0 = no effectiveness, 1 = minimal effectiveness, 2 = mildly effective, 3 = moderately effective, 4 = very effective, 5 = extremely effective)

Evaluating Your IPE Practice

Now that you have practiced these IPE skills for a week, practice them over and over until they're second nature. Use the following questions to review your experience, noting what works, and what you might need to tweak to enhance your practice.

Which set of IPE skills do you find the most natural to you? _____

_____

_____

Which set of IPE skills do you find the most difficult to practice? _____

_____

_____

Describe situations in which you practiced your skills: _____

_____

_____

Describe any rehearsals you practiced with friends: _____

_____

_____

Describe emotions that you experienced as you practiced these skills: _____

_____

_____

Describe any obstacles to your practice of IPE skills and what you can do to remove them:

_____

_____

Describe your plans to continue to practice your IPE skills, including situations in which you can use them (work, school, home, coffee shop): _____

_____

_____

CHAPTER 13

Intimacy Skills

In the last chapter, we talked about relationship skills in general. In this one, we'll focus more closely on the skills involved in an intimate relationship, which usually means with your partner or spouse. (To save space, I'll use "partner" to refer to the person you share a committed relationship with, regardless of formal status.)

Your best efforts to relate with others can break down when you or the other person become dichotomous in your thinking and your attempts to solve problems. You can recognize dichotomous thinking if you notice thoughts that reflect these qualities:

- Either-or

- All-or-nothing

- Me versus them

- Willful (overcontrol or passivity)

There are many reasons you might get caught up in dichotomous thinking. It could be an old habit. Strong emotions often trigger old and impulsive habits, even habits of thought. Or the other person also may be engaging in dichotomous ways of thinking and arguing. Taking the dichotomous route leads to a sort of relational combat in which one of you must win and one must lose. When discussions or arguments become combative you may not make much progress in resolving the issue at hand while also maintaining your relationship.

In contrast to dichotomous thinking, the dialectical thinking path has these qualities:

- Both/and

- Asks, "What's being left out?"

- Me *and* you (us)

- Willing (open to the relationship, participatory)

Dichotomous versus Dialectical (Sample)

Here's an example of a commonplace relationship conflict that was made worse by purely dichotomous thinking.

Relationship conflict: I don't like it that Sally spends so much money on clothes and styling her hair. Sally says that she needs these things for work, but it's several times a month, and that's just too much. She becomes defensive when I bring this up.

What's at stake for us? I think we're spending too much money on her shopping addiction, when we have loans and bills to pay. Sally denies that her purchases are impulsive, and she says that she believes she needs the professional hair care and shoes for work and social functions, so that she can look good.

My feelings about the conflict: I get angry because I feel like she doesn't listen to me. I just want her to take our finances more seriously. I also want her to know how hard I work for the money that she uses to buy the shoes, since I earn more than she does. Sometimes I'm just pissed that we can't agree on this.

My spouse's/partner's feelings about the conflict (include hints and signals): I think she gets sad since she gets tearful when I complain about her spending. When I raise my voice she also raises her voice, so she sometimes seems angry. She says that I don't value how hard she tries to look attractive for work and for me, and that I don't want her to have anything at all.

Dichotomous thinking in our conflict:

- Either-or

There seem to be some thoughts such as either she can spend whatever she wants on fashion or she can't spend any money on these things.

- All-or-nothing

I don't know about Sally, but I have been thinking either she can or can't spend money on fashion, or if she does she'll spend too much.

Dichotomy versus Dialectical Practice

Now let's apply the above analysis to a relationship conflict of your own. Think of a conflict that exists in your relationship, and analyze it the same way, with this difference: Once you identify your dichotomous thinking, go a step beyond it and see if you can think of a dialectical resolution. Use the following worksheet to remind yourself to introduce dialectical thinking into the relational equation.

Relationship conflict: _____

_____

_____

_____

What's at stake for us? _____

_____

_____

_____

My feelings about the conflict: _____

_____

_____

_____

My partner's feelings about the conflict (include hints and signals): _____

_____

_____

_____

Dichotomous thinking in our conflict:

- Either-or

_____

_____

- All-or-nothing

_____

_____

- Me or you

_____

_____

- Willfulness (overcontrol or overly passive)

_____

_____

Apply dialectical thinking:

- Both/and

_____

_____

- Ask, "What's being left out?"

_____

_____

- Me and you (us)

_____

_____

- Willingness (participate, reciprocity, open)

_____

_____

What was the outcome?

After applying the dialectical strategies, describe the outcome. Describe how you may have felt differently, whether or not it seemed as though the two of you were more collaborative and less combative, and the overall difference these strategies seem to make to you.

_____

_____

Asking for Repairs

What happens if you offend someone close to you? What if they offend you? In both cases, action is called for, specifically, *making repairs*.

As you practice noticing and validating your emotional experiences, you will also practice validating your emotions with respect to relationships with others. This includes how you respond to them and how their behaviors trigger your emotion ("make" you feel), especially with respect to how you believe they are treating you.

There will there be times when you will offend others and need to apologize and make repairs. Others will offend you and need to make repairs in turn. Either way, this practice requires assertiveness. If you have a relationship that you want to keep but is being threatened by the other person's behaviors, you have to take these steps: identify these problem behaviors; tell the other person that you want to keep the relationship; and ask them to change the behaviors so the relationship can survive.

To make this real, complete the worksheet below, using real examples of offensive behavior you may have experienced, and describing how repairs were (or weren't) made.

Making Repairs

Situation: _____

_____

_____

_____

Damage or offense to me: _____

_____

_____

_____

Identify specific behavior(s) that you find offensive: _____

_____

_____

_____

Do you believe the other person is willing and/or able to provide repairs? _____

_____

_____

_____

What obstacles do you foresee to asking for repairs (worry thoughts, self-invalidation)?

_____

_____

_____

Following up: What was the outcome of your request for repairs?

Describe the other person's receptivity to your request for repairs: _____

_____

_____

_____

Did you get what you wanted or did you need to negotiate? _____

_____

_____

_____

Describe how or why this repair is satisfactory enough to continue the relationship:

_____

_____

_____

Bringing Mindfulness to Relationships

Let's take a look at how to apply your mindfulness skills to relationships. Many times when conflict arises in relationships it's due to misunderstanding. Misunderstanding often comes from the assumption that you're right, or that you know what the other person's motives are, or they can come from what Albert Ellis (1994) calls *false generalizations, unrealistic conclusions,* and *self-defeating conclusions.* Let me give you an example of each.

False generalizations. This is when you think you are your behavior—when you turn what you *do* (even if only once) into what you *are.* If you spill your coffee all over your new pants in front of a group of people, you're a klutz. If you're late to meetings you must be slow or you must be lazy, and always will be.

Unrealistic conclusions. This is thinking that you'll never change behaviors that you dislike about yourself. Example: "I ate the whole bag of chips last night. I'll never be able to control myself."

Self-defeating conclusions. These thoughts reflect an expectation for hopelessness in your efforts to change how you relate with others. They might go something like, "Since I'm worthless and lazy, what's the use of trying to change anything?"

In relationships you may find that you apply these assumptions and thoughts both to yourself and to the people you try to relate with, especially where there are longstanding patterns of behaviors that cause pain for you. Often that pain comes from your not getting what you want from the other person (respect, money, protection, praise from your boss, etc.). But if you hold rigidly to these beliefs you will find that some of your emotional pain will be exacerbated. The stronger you hold to them the more influence they will have on your emotional responses in relationships.

These rigid, self-defeating thoughts are non-dialectical in nature, and reflect all-or-nothing thinking. You can use dialectical reasoning to combat them. As Albert Ellis says, it's important that you become aware of these thoughts, and that you not only mildly challenge them, but actively argue against these beliefs in an engaged manner in order to get to the balance you need.

Marriage and Emotion

John Gottman and his colleagues at the University of Washington have spent a good deal of time studying factors that predict divorce in married couples. Unhappily married couples that eventually divorced followed a pattern, says Gottman, of "a certain downward spiral of interactions, emotions, and attitudes that leads to the disintegration of their mar-riages." Four elements were most often at fault, which he calls "The Four Horsemen of the Apocalypse" (Gottman and Silver 1994; 1999):

1. Criticism

2. Contempt

3. Defensiveness

4. Stonewalling

There's a reason why I'm including this analysis in the skills part of the book, by the way. For the emotionally sensitive person, general IPE skills work very well in most set-tings, but marriage or a committed relationship is quite different from work, school, etc. And while you may instinctively apply IPE skills in that relationship, you may want to tune them to a slightly different frequency, to watch for approaching horsemen, and use modified IPE skills against them.

The following material will help you to see if any of these problems apply to your relationship or marriage. And while these ideas are applicable to committed couples, they are also useful for divorced or separated couples who need to cooperate in child rearing. As you read about the four horsemen, consider whether any are present in your relation-ship with your partner, and how you might apply IPE skills to counter and eject these apocalyptic monsters.

1. **Criticism.** Criticism isn't the same as complaining, says Gottman. Complaining addresses a specific behavior; criticism is the act of making negative remarks about your partner's personality or character in a blaming or accusatory way. Contrasted to criticism, complaints are directed toward specific and observable behavior.

2. **Contempt.** Contempt is similar to criticism, but goes far beyond it. Contempt *intends* to emotionally and psychologically injure the other person. It's a sort of emotional assassin. When you're overrun with negative emotion, you may begin to think of your partner in demeaning ways. The longer you hold these thoughts, the harder it becomes to remember the positive qualities that first attracted you to them in the first place. Kindness can become swallowed up by contempt if it isn't checked. Contempt is dangerous to a relationship because it corrodes the things that bond you. Like a powerful acid, intentional insults and injuries weaken the bonds of affection, shared goals, and love.

3. **Defensiveness.** You're likely to be defensive when you feel under emotional assault. That's normal and adaptive. But if partners don't listen to each other, and don't notice what they're saying, they can become mindlessly engaged in a mari-tal siege. When you become defensive you may make excuses or deny your responsibility or your role in creating problems that you face as a couple.

4. **Stonewalling.** Stonewalling is simply shutting down. For the stonewalling per-son, it may be that the situation has become too intense for them and stonewall-ing, like dissociating, helps bring emotions down to a manageable level. The

problem is that while stonewalling can be effective in bringing emotions into control, it also circumvents intimacy. This horseman is usually associated with male communication-avoidant behavior, but women engage in it as well in emotionally charged situations.

These four attitudes are present in nearly all relationships. However, the difference between relationships that are on the road toward divorce or breakup and those who will survive, according to Gottman's research, is in the presence of repairs. Where people make repairs, they also usually share tenderness, affection, and positive emotions. These help protect the relationship against the corrosive powers of the four elements above.

You can use your mindfulness skills to notice or be aware if the horsemen are present in your relationship, and you can use your IPE skills to counter them. And if you're intentional about making repairs, your relationship won't be needlessly ravaged.

Adapting Relationship Assumptions

One element of DBT that can be quite helpful in treating difficult problems is its development of new assumptions about people and their problems, and then making these new assumptions explicit. I suggest you consider adopting for your relationship the assumptions that we first listed in the book's introduction. You may want to sit down with your partner, discuss them, and then keep them handy as a reminder. When you need to have tough discussions, pull these assumptions out and put them on the table or keep them in hand as a guide for your discussions. They will help you avoid or unseat the four deadly horsemen.

1. Both of us are doing the best we can, given our respective histories and biological uniqueness.

2. Both of can always do better. We can learn, grow, change, adapt, and become more skillful.

3. Both of want to do better. We both want to maintain and enhance this relationship, even though our negative emotions and mindless patterns have gotten in the way.

4. Both of us have to do better, try harder, and apply our skills to every relevant situation that has the potential to either corrode or promote our intimacy.

5. Neither one of us may have caused *all* of the problems in our relationship, and we both have to work together to solve them anyway.

Making Relationship Agreements

Just you can make the underlying assumptions about your relationship explicit, it can help to make certain agreements explicit as well. Here are six specific agreements that you may find useful:

- Dialectical Agreement

- Consultation-to-Partner Agreement

- Consistency Agreement

- Observing-Limits Agreement

- Empathy Agreement

- Fallibility Agreement

Like the assumptions, you may either use these agreements as is, or adapt them to better fit your relationship. Let's look at them in some detail.

Dialectical Agreement

This agreement means that you will strive to be balanced in your relationship, that you will try to walk the middle path between extremes of emotions, behavior, and thinking. It means that you recognize that neither one of you "owns" the complete, comprehensive, and exhaustive truth about your relationship, or is ever 100 percent correct about a situation or problem.

None of us possess a perspective that accounts for every factor that goes into creating or solving a problem. So when you face a problem, you agree to ask yourselves the question, "What's being left out?" You need to do this individually as well as together. When your partner seems to be acting strangely or bizarrely, or is just plain rude, you can ask yourself, "What is it that I am leaving out of this situation?" or "What is it that I don't see or feel that factors in?"

Consultation-to-Partner Agreement

With this agreement you're pledging to one another not to use a go-between to solve your problems. It does *not* mean you shouldn't or can't seek counseling, because psychotherapy can often help relationships. But if you go into couples counseling, your therapist or counselor can't solve your problems for you, and shouldn't become your go-between. At most they might be a coach to facilitate change through observation and feedback in sessions.

Make sure that your mother-in-law isn't the one telling you what's on your partner's mind. And don't be the one who goes to a friend, minister, or relative just to complain about your partner. Ask those people for constructive ideas, but bring them home. Remember, only you and your partner can solve the problems you face.

Consistency Agreement

This agreement means that the two of you don't have to be emotionally or behaviorally identical. You don't have to like the same foods, drinks, books, or even weather. Neither one of you has to have identical problem-solving skills. Likewise, your relationships with others don't have to be the same. Let's suppose that in a certain marriage the wife sees her mother once a week, and the husband sees his mother once a month. The wife needs to accept that her husband's behavior doesn't mean that he's a cold person or a bad son. And the husband should abandon any judgments that his wife's more frequent visits mean she's enmeshed or a mama's girl.

Observing-Limits Agreement

You can call this a his-and-hers agreement to define one's own limits. It means that as a couple you need to communicate with one another about what you need and what is non-negotiable (such as adultery, compulsive gambling, not working, etc.).

Empathy Agreement

This one speaks for itself. It's simply agreeing to do your level best to try to see life through the eyes of the other person. Or to put it another way, to walk a mile in their shoes.

Fallibility Agreement

We are all jackasses from time to time. This agreement just makes it explicit so that you're not shocked when you or your partner blows it or violates all of the above agreements.

Keeping These Agreements Explicit

At the beginning of the book we talked about assumptions I made about you, the reader. You may recall that I recommended keeping these assumptions explicit by posting them somewhere where you're likely to see them. In the interest of enhancing your relationship, I suggest you do the same thing with these relationship agreements. To get you started you may want to copy the following reminder to keep somewhere in your house, car, day planner, or on the fridge or bedroom closet door. When you need to have important discussions that are usually heated and emotional you can sit down with a copy of these assumptions, using them to guide your discussion.

Assumptions and Agreements: United We Stand

We are united in mortal combat against the Four Horsemen of criticism, contempt, defensiveness, and stonewalling.

Because we love another, with all of our respective foibles, failures, glory, and beauty, we will assume the following about one another:

1. Both of us are doing the best we can, given our respective histories and biological uniqueness.

2. Both of can always do better. We can learn, grow, change, adapt, and become more skillful.

3. Both of want to do better. We both want to maintain and enhance this relationship, even though our negative emotions and mindless patterns have gotten in the way.

4. Both of us have to do better, try harder, and apply our skills to every relevant situation that can corrode our intimacy, or promote it.

5. Neither of us may have caused *all* of the problems in our relationship, and we both have to work together to solve them anyway.

In order to make these assumptions a living reality in our relationship, we pledge to adhere to the following agreements:

1. Dialectical Thinking Agreement

As a couple, we agree to practice more flexible thinking, trying to be aware of the polarities and dichotomous thinking that lead to disagreements. We agree that neither of us singularly or absolutely owns the truth, even though we will both have our opinions on matters.

2. Consultation-to-Partner Agreement

Ultimately, we must consult with one another to sort out problems in our relationship. If we seek outside wisdom or input, we will go to outside sources to get support and help, and not to put down or criticize each other. That's trading gossip, not seeking help. When we do get good advice, we will bring it back to each other to talk about what we'll do to change.

3. Consistency Agreement

We agree that we aren't required to share the same tastes, preferences, or limits. Just because one of us likes sushi doesn't mean that we both must like sushi. The same applies to action movies and romantic comedies. We also agree to accept that each of us will behave somewhat differently from one situation to another depending on vulnerabilities and other events. What is fine on Saturday may not work on Monday, and we accept that. We agree that each of us will act differently toward the other depending on situation, context, and roles. Each of us will set their own rules to a reasonable degree.

4. Observing Limits Agreement

Each of us is responsible for setting their own limits, which may change from time to time. When one of us is ill the other may extend their limits to do all the home chores, and then relinquish them when the ill party recovers. Each of us will have different limits for what we will tolerate from children, friends, or family. We agree to not set those for one another but be willing to openly discuss and accept them.

5. Empathy Agreement

We agree to try to understand each other's behavior in light of the other's history and skills. We agree to try to put off judgmental attitudes and try to see life from the other's perspective. When we're faced with our partner's problematic behaviors, we agree to try to interpret them in a nonpejorative or nonjudgmental way. We agree to allow each other to hold each of us to these agreements.

6. Fallibility Agreement

We agree that, being fallible human beings, both of us will invariably blow these agreements on occasion. When we do, we will help each other to return to the agreements to continue building a relationship that we enjoy as a whole.

CHAPTER 14

Survival and Acceptance

Emotions can be painful, and if you sometimes suffer from intense and overwhelming sadness or anger, it's important to learn how to experience your emotions skillfully. Otherwise, when you're deep in emotion you may engage in impulsive behaviors that make things worse—overeating, binge drinking, or cutting yourself—and will keep you from your goals.

Distress tolerance skills are designed to help you bear pain skillfully (Linehan 1993). This doesn't mean to get rid of it. Many of my clients are disappointed when we first discuss distress tolerance when they learn that I don't have a method of ridding their lives of pain. But they also quickly understand the importance of these skills when they grasp the truth of the statement, "Pain is inevitable." Living in this life means that we're all subject to bruised knees, bumped heads, and broken hearts.

Distress tolerance can be broken down into two major and equally important categories: *crisis survival skills* and *acceptance skills*. Because I know of so many very specific ways to help you get through crises, I'll spend most of this chapter listing crisis survival skills. At the end of the chapter I'll say a few words about acceptance and willingness, and the importance of learning from pain.

The following skills will help you tolerate your pain or change the source of the pain and buffer yourself against it, so you become more emotionally resilient.

Crisis Survival Skills

From the following list, check off situations that are crisis situations for you, including emotions you feel in a crisis:

☐ Fired from job

☐ Significant other leaves you/breakup of romance

☐ Work colleague gets credit for a your idea or your work

☐ Stood up for a date

☐ Fail a test at school

☐ Child runs away from home

☐ Someone disapproves of your behavior

☐ Spending the weekend alone

☐ Overate

☐ Didn't exercise

☐ Feeling lonely

☐ Sad

☐ Bored

☐ Embarrassed

☐ Scared

☐ Angry

☐ Other: _____

Crisis Survival Strategies

Crisis skills are concrete, tangible activities you can engage in when you find yourself in crisis and it isn't possible at that moment to change things for the better. These skills can help you survive bad situations without making them worse. Each is related to what we've already established about emotional resilience and intelligence. These are strategies for getting your whole self engaged in skillful responses to situations. One of the best is to use *distractions*.

You can distract yourself in many ways, so the following are just suggestions. In each group of activities, you will surely think of many others. Here are my basic suggestions when you're in crisis:

- Get physically or mentally active

- Reach out to other people

- Remind yourself that things could be worse

- Use opposite emotions

- Use "setting aside" thoughts

- Energize your thinking

- Seek out powerful physical sensations

- Soothe yourself

Get Active

Find things to do that can preoccupy you, or require your full attention and so pull your mind out of distressing thoughts and keep you from dwelling on how bad things are.

- Work out with weights

- Do yoga

- Build a model

- Attend a religious service

- Go window-shopping

- Play computer games

- Play solitaire

- Meet a friend for a game of chess

- Attend hearings in public courts

- Go to a museum

- Chop wood

- Landscape

- Clean your home

- Make a to-do list

- Read a book

- Make a meal for a friend or a loved one

- Go on a date

- Plan for the future

- Write a mission statement for your life

- Memorize a poem or quotations
- Practice a foreign language
- Send e-mail
- Search the Internet for information about emotions
- Organize your closet
- Do your homework
- Make a list of people you want to send holiday cards to
- Write letters to friends, family, politicians
- Write a letter to the editor
- Debate an issue with someone
- Visit shut-ins
- Take inventory of your wardrobe
- Write about the way you would like your life to be

Give of Yourself

- Do volunteer work (library, hospital, church, etc.)
- Donate money to a cause you believe in
- Write a note of appreciation or encouragement to someone you know
- Send a thank-you note to someone
- Start a petition for a cause or political issue you think is worthy
- Meet someone for a meal, and pay the check when they don't expect it
- Bake goodies for someone
- Send out cards to loved ones
- Visit someone who is sick
- Make a meal for a friend or two
- Throw a surprise birthday party
- Send flowers anonymously
- Buy someone a subscription to their favorite publication
- Take a friend to a spa
- Buy a gift certificate for someone else
- Pick flowers for someone

- Say prayers for the well-being of others

- Make a card from scratch and send it

- Write a letter of reference

Remember, It Could Be Worse

No matter how bad things get, they could always be worse. Is that a cliché? Yes, and it's true. For those of who can walk, it's nice to have legs that we take for granted, for those who can't walk but can see it's nice to have sight. For those who are blind at least they have hearing. For those who are deaf and blind at least they can learn to communicate with those around them, as Helen Keller proved. And at least she had her freedom and wasn't imprisoned for her political or religious beliefs, as has happened to other people. It can be always be worse.

Think about the ways it could be worse and be grateful that it's not worse than it is. Also comparisons can reveal to us others who are going through some of the same issues and challenges and may be doing as well as we are. We can take comfort in knowing that we're not alone. This can dispel the idea that the world and the cosmos are out to get us, since much of what befalls us also befalls others. And then there are those who are facing similar challenges but are coping less well. We can take pride and comfort that we're doing relatively well compared to some folks. The idea isn't to gloat over others, or to feel bad about being a bratty spoilsport when others with less seem more mature. Look at what is instructive about each comparison, and how they promote your well-being and move you to increase your wisdom in living with your emotions.

- Compare yourself to others who have less money than you do

- Compare yourself with those who are coping the same or worse than you

- Watch soap operas or daytime talk shows

- Read stories about people who have lost everything

- Watch news stories about catastrophes, loss, and accidents

- Compare yourself with those who are homeless

- Be thankful for what you do have

Create Opposite Emotions

It's important here to choose activities that create emotions other than those that you're feeling. So if you're sad, do things that make you feel upbeat or happy. The choices will be personal, and may be quite idiosyncratic. When I'm feeling low for example, I like to listen to a wide range of music: Vivaldi, *The Four Seasons*; Mozart, *Eine Kleine Nachtmusik*; Wagner, *Flight of the Valkyries*; and—for a change of pace, as it were—Nancy Sinatra singing "These Boots Are Made for Walkin.'"

- Read emotional books or stories that trigger different emotions

- Listen to emotional music such as anthems, hymnals, fight songs, or anything uplifting

- Watch inspirational and emotional movies

- Read joke books

- Read funny greeting cards

- Read inspirational literature

- Read how-to books

- Read religious and spiritual literature

"Setting Aside" Thoughts

Use your imagination or thoughts to interrupt your current thoughts if they are distressing, or are restarting intense negative emotion. Telling yourself that your problems will still be around later may make this easier (in case you're worried they will disappear). Cut yourself some slack for now. You don't have to worry about your worries not being around to worry about. Give yourself a break from troubles.

- Mentally leave your distressing situation

- Intentionally block out distressing thoughts

- Think about pleasant things

- Remember happier times

- Think about people who have been kind to you

- Censor your rumination

- Think about an activity that you enjoy such as tennis, golfing, camping, painting, etc.

- Build an imaginary wall between yourself and the problem

- Think about the successes of friends, children, family that make you smile

- Imagine that you're in a beautiful location, surrounded by lush trees and bright flowers

- Put your problems in an imaginary box, and place that box on an imaginary shelf

- Think about future plans for work, writing, marriage, etc.

Energize Your Thinking

Use other thoughts to crowd your short-term memory. This can derail obsessing and negative thinking related to distress, anger, or depression. For example, if you're having steady thoughts about something that went wrong (a breakup, being fired, etc.) and these thoughts are feeding into emotional dysregulation, think about something that really engrosses your attention. Try to think about things that really take up your brain space as it were. Think about pleasant times, do mental exercises—whatever works.

- Count to 10, 50, or 100

- Watch something engrossing on TV

- Read a suspenseful novel or mystery

- Work crossword or jigsaw puzzles

- Work logic problems

- Try to understand obscure poetry

- Look at a piece of art and try to understand the artist's conception

- Read in a foreign language

- Count tiles in a floor or a ceiling

- Write out your solution to a political or social problem

- Read biographies

- Memorize and recite prayers, poetry, or songs

- Memorize facts about topics that interest you

- Use the Internet to build a resources file

- Try to remember every detail of a beautiful day you had

- Try to recall the features of faces you haven't seen in while

Seek Powerful Sensations

Strong physical sensations can interfere with the physiological component of your current negative emotion and thereby short-circuit the emotional process. As you know from earlier chapters, emotions prime your body for action. So if you can interfere with the current emotion as it's priming you can prevent emotional overheating and interrupt chains of behavior and feeling that could otherwise lead to impulsive acts.

Strong physical sensations may also interrupt physiological action urges, such as the urge to harm yourself or other people, to eat or drink to excess, and a host of other behaviors you may be trying to eliminate. By using your physical senses to interrupt destructive patterns, you will be engaging your whole self to change, not just your brain or will-power, but your body, too. Here are some suggestions for sensation-seekers:

- Hold ice cubes very tightly in your hands

- Eat tangy Popsicles

- Suck on or eat lemons or limes

- Take a very hot or very cold shower, or alternate hot and cold water

- Snap a rubber band on your wrist

- Drink bitter coffee

- Listen to hard and loud music

- Suck on very tart or sour candies, letting them melt in your mouth

- Squeeze stress balls

- Do isometric exercises

- Do push-ups

- Put ice or a frozen item to your forehead

- Fill a tub with very cold water, get in, and stay in till it's tepid

- Plunge your bare feet into a bucket of icy water

- Smell pungent cheeses

- Wear a heat pack or ice pack

- Bite into an onion

Self-Soothing

When you feel distressed, find a way to soothe yourself. Don't wait for others to soothe you, although you may want to think about people you can call on to soothe you later. The more things you can think of to do and practice in any given moment the better, since it's unrealistic to expect that others will always be available when you need them. To self-soothe you will want to use activities that engage one or more of the five senses: vision, hearing, smell, taste, and touch (Linehan 1993).

Vision

Think about all the things you can do or think you can do, or find yourself interested in making accessible to you. Focus on using your sense of sight to see beauty, peaceful scenes, and art. Order your living and work space to reduce any visual chaos or stress.

- Hang pictures on your walls

- Buy and look at a beautiful painting, print, or poster

- Buy a decorative centerpiece

- Put up seasonal decorations

- Look at trees, grass, or plants

- Look at rivers, ponds, or fountains

- Look at photo books or magazines

- Watch nature shows

- Look at art or photography books

- Look at shop window displays

- Go to the zoo and look at the animals

- Watch the sunrise or sunset

- Watch a thunderstorm

- Drive or walk around your town and look at architecture

- Paint a room in your house a soothing color

- Look at magazines

- Go look at the ocean

- Drive across a prairie or up a mountain

- Look at art books

Hearing

With the emphasis on soothing, you want to find sounds that relax you, calm you, or reassure you. Heavy metal may be great for distraction, but for self-soothing you want chamber music or ballads.

- Listen to classical music

- Listen to mellow instrumental music

- Buy a "noise" machine with nature sounds

- Play a musical instrument

- Ask a friend to play an instrument for you

- Sing to yourself

- Ask a friend to sing to you or with you

- Listen to relaxation or meditation tapes

- Listen to affirmation tapes

- Listen to books on tape

- Turn on a fan, air purifier, or anything else that makes white noise

- Listen to recordings of Gregorian chants

- Hum a tune

- Whistle

- Have a friend read to you

- Call a friend

- Call a toll-free line to hear a human voice

- Call a weather, time, and temperature line

- Call joke lines

- Read out loud

Smell

Either fill your environment with delicious or beautiful smells, or, if you can't do that then take yourself somewhere that you can experience smells that bring delight. You may find smells that trigger positive memories that will likely help you relax.

- Burn incense or scented candles

- Go to a bakery or café and stand around, taking in the smells

- Rub scented oil or lotion over your body

- Bake fresh bread or brownies

- Spray air freshener around your home

- Put on cologne or perfume

- Apply scented aftershave gel or lotion after shaving

- Apply fresh deodorant/antiperspirant

- Wash your hair with fruit-scented shampoo (strawberry, banana, etc.)

- Notice the smell of freshly cut grass

- Take a whiff of pungent cheese (Limburger, Gouda, blue cheese)

- Build a fire in your fireplace, notice the smell

- Use air freshener plug-ins

- Smell flowers

- Go to wooded area and notice the smells

- Sample perfumes and colognes at local department store

- Smell fresh laundry

Touch

Remember that you're human, and as a human you need touch like everyone else. Touch is very nurturing and it triggers endorphins to release in your body, giving you a sense of well-being and connection to others. Touch is also a form of communication and can be social, but if you are alone there are strategies to use touch.

- Get a massage

- Hug someone

- Hug a tree

- Go for a swim

- Take a long and luxurious bath

- Rub oil or lotion all over your body

- Put clean sheets on your bed and climb in

- Put on silk pajamas or underwear

- Take a long hot shower

- Notice how the wind feels blowing across your face and body

- Massage your hand, foot, arm, or leg

- Give or get a back rub

- Rub your temples and forehead

- Squish your toes in mud

- Walk barefoot through sand, mud, or grass

- Soak your feet in warm water, a pool, or a stream

- Go skinny-dipping

- Hold hands

Taste

When you're feeling distressed, it's wise to avoid too much sugar, caffeine, and alcohol. Sugar or caffeine can make you edgy, and alcohol can impair your judgment and impulse control, making you more vulnerable to the negative emotional state you might be experiencing. So pay attention to your needs, your body, and your medical issues. Know what will soothe you, instead of trigger you.

- Slowly eat your favorite food, savoring every bite

- Slowly and mindfully drink a warm drink, feeling its warmth entering you

- Eat hot toast

- Eat peppermint or cinnamon candy, slowly

- Drink chocolate milk

- Chew your favorite gum, or try a new one

- Have some heated water with lemon squeezed into it

- Drink herbal tea

- Drink warm milk

- Have a bowl of your favorite soup

- Make a salad with green leafy lettuce, green and black olives, onions, and feta cheese

- Have an ice cream cone or make an ice cream sundae

- Sample foods at your local deli

Obstacles to Self-Soothing

When some people are first introduced to the idea of self-soothing, they find the skills very hard to do. That's because they're basically convinced that either they don't deserve to experience soothing, or that it's a selfish practice. They may feel guilty even thinking about being kind and gentle to themselves. If this is the case for you, it's important to identify any thoughts that might interfere with your self-soothing. Guilt around this will be an obstacle, and obstacles can be overcome.

On the following list of beliefs, check all the obstacles of thought you identify with as your own, or add others at the end of the list. After you're done, consider other practical obstacles on the resources list and what you can do to get around them.

Belief Obstacles

☐ I don't deserve to feel good

☐ I don't deserve compassion or kindness, even from myself

☐ Self-soothing is a wasteful indulgence

☐ I shouldn't have to soothe myself

☐ I don't really know what self-soothing is

☐ I don't think soothing will help me

☐ I don't have time for self-soothing

☐ Whenever I try to self-soothe

☐ I think others should soothe me

☐ If others don't soothe me I shouldn't soothe myself

☐ A man might say: self-soothing is for women

☐ I can't stand the shame I feel when I self–soothe

☐ I can't soothe myself

☐ If I try to self-soothe I'll just become angry or sad

☐ Other: _____

Self-Cutting: Phoebe

When I met her, Phoebe had been cutting herself for nearly ten years. She started in middle school and continued into her college years. Whenever she became emotionally escalated she found the pain unbearable, and got relief in cutting. This seemed very strange to her friends and family, and to some therapists she worked with. They couldn't imagine the degree of relief it brought for her.

When Phoebe began to address her cutting in DBT, she discovered that cutting gave her relief and distraction from her emotional pain. The secondary fallout for her was a sense of shame for losing control, and from the realization that her friends and family saw her cutting as manipulative or bizarre. As she worked in DBT, she reached a point of willingness to try practical methods to interrupt the old patterns that preceded and followed her episodes of cutting.

As she increased her awareness to sensations, Phoebe began to recognize sooner when she had urges to cut and started to use ice to interrupt them. She was incredulous when I first recommended this, but I explained that strong physical sensations often "short-circuit" the usual feelings preceding cutting. They also powerfully interrupt thoughts associated with cutting, and by doing so ultimately interrupt strong negative emotions.

After months of going back to this practice over and over again, she began to notice that she didn't have to cut and that in fact, her urges for cutting became diminished. She did have lapses and did cut. But instead of writing herself off as a failure, she compared cutting episodes with situations in which she didn't cut and realized that not only was she gaining more control over herself, but also that she preferred the results of not cutting to cutting. She continued in her success as she also added other skills such as observing and describing, breathing, and acts of self-soothing.

Phoebe learned that much of what triggered her intense emotional experiences wasn't entirely a result of her inherent weaknesses. She often left issues alone until they had become larger-than-life. So she began to tackle interpersonal problems head-on and practiced assertiveness, which led to her problems becoming more manageable. She still had problems, but they were different in scale.

In about six months Phoebe nearly eliminated her cutting. Within a year she was able to look back at least four months solid without any self-mutilating behaviors. She now says she has gone a whole year without cutting and continues to use her DBT skills to the best of her abilities.

Resources Obstacles

☐ I don't have a lot of money

☐ I don't have a lot of time

☐ I don't have lotions, creams, candles

☐ I don't have transportation

☐ I don't have a big bathtub

☐ I can't go to a spa

☐ I don't know where to go to self-soothe

☐ I lack privacy at home

☐ Other: _____

Problem: I don't have a lot of money.

Solution: Work with what you have at home or your neighborhood.

- Use your bathtub or shower for your soothing bath or shower. Even if you don't have bubble bath or bath crystals, soaking in a tub of hot water relaxes the muscles and feels wonderful.

- Do a load of laundry, including bedclothes. Put them on your bed right from the line or the dryer and climb into bed as soon as possible to feel the clean, warm sheets.

- Clean your home or bedroom. When you're done, sit and look at the peace that order can bring to you.

- Massage your feet, hands, and legs. Check out a book on massage from your local library so you learn professional techniques to use on yourself.

- Cook a can of soup and let the aroma waft through your house. Be mindful to the delicious smell.

- Look at the trees, grass, plants, or flowers in your yard or park. Observe and describe how looking at these soothes you.

- Use your local library to look at picture books and magazines.

- Walk near or into restaurants, cafés, or bakeries, taking in the smells of foods and coffee.

Problem: I don't have a lot of time.

Solution: You must make time. These skills are too important to you to just let them go without trying. People who never get around to exercising often say, "I have no time." But then those who do exercise regularly say, "I don't have time to exercise, but I make the time anyway." The same is true for all these skills, as a matter of fact. No one *has* time, but everyone can *make* time.

- Write self-soothing practices into your day planner, scheduling soothing sessions. List soothing activities that you will, or have, put into your planner.

- Put specific self-soothing activities on your to-do list.

- Make verbal commitments to others that you will practice specific skills each day.

- Cut back on other activities (e.g., too much TV or video games). Make a list of activities that you do too much. List specific TV programs you will give up.

- Set up agreements with a therapist or friend to report to after you practice self-soothing.

- Begin with brief but specific practices; start with fifteen minutes. Later, plan a whole day.

Problem: I don't have transportation.

Solution: Look for things you can do without transportation. Make a list of things you can do at home, use public transportation if that is available in your area, or ask friends and family for an occasional ride.

Make an Emergency Self-Soothing Kit

You can't always predict when an emotional emergency will strike, but you know that it will happen inevitably, so make preparations now. All of the distraction and soothing techniques mentioned above help to get thoughts going somewhere other than deeper into rumination, and they get the body and brain forcibly reoriented.

I often urge my clients to make a sort of "emergency kit" that includes items that they have found effective to get through a crisis without making it worse. They put a basket, box, or bag around the house where they can easily access these things. (It's important to be able to find the kit easily, because it's hard to think calmly when you're exceptionally angry or in great turmoil.)

Here's an example of what you might place in such a kit:

- Lilac or almond body lotion

- Classical CD

- Rabbit's foot or worry stone

- Incense

- A few chocolates

- A tacky tabloid newspaper

After creating your soothing kit, making some other changes around your home can also help you be prepared. This is especially important if you struggle with self-harm behaviors, such as cutting. You will want to strongly grab your body's and brain's attention so you might emphasize strong physical sensations.

Think about any items that you have available to you, or that you can afford to put together. Some of the ideas may not suit you, but don't disregard them. They came from people going through much of the same thing as you. Be willing to try something new. Remember, distress tolerance isn't about solving life's deepest and most profound problems; it's about surviving intense emotional crises without making things worse.

Put a few ice cubes in sandwich bags. When you begin to feel very dysregulated go to the freezer, grab a bag of ice, and squeeze tightly. Sandwich bags will keep dripping to a minimum, but if you don't care about having some water on the floor, try holding the ice without the baggies.

Keep lemon concentrate or lemon juice available in the fridge. Lick, drink, or directly taste these without diluting them. They can be quite potent in flavor, and be strong distractions. You can also cut up some fresh lemon, lime, or grapefruit wedges and put them in a plastic container in your fridge. When necessary, get them out, bite down into them, and feel those taste buds come to life!

Keep frozen cranberries, blueberries, or strawberries on hand. Get them out and chew slowly, feeling the cold and noticing as the tart or sweet flavors explode in your mouth. Keep orange Popsicles handy, and use them the same way.

These are all examples of things my clients have tried for themselves and taught me about. Whatever items you select, make sure you know where to find them. Place them where they make sense to you to go and look. You take a bubble bath in the bathroom; so don't put the bubble bath soap in the garage.

Develop a Crisis Network

It is important that you find outside help rather than always trying to shoulder your burdens alone. For periods of crisis, you will want to have professionals, friends, and family available to you by phone or pager who are willing to provide support and intervention as appropriate and according to role.

For example, you will expect a therapist who provides crisis coverage after hours to provide professionally trained and informed intervention. Your friends and family aren't your mental health providers. It's best to establish that with your network members up front. Be sure that you understand what you can expect from each member so you don't become needlessly frustrated with laypeople who can't provide professional services.

On the flip side, if you have professionals available, either your own therapist or by way of a local crisis line, understand that these individuals can't be your friends. So if the professionals engage you with a style that seems "clinically distant," remember that your goal in a crisis is to get help, not to develop friendships. You'll also want to discuss your need for crisis support up front, inviting each willing member of your network to participate in their respective capacity, according to the nature of their relationship to you.

Flexibly and compassionately let these people change their minds later. If your network members communicate a desire to change their status, for whatever reason, be willing to graciously let them do so. Thank them for having been supportive to you and ask if there are other ways they can be generally supportive, such as sharing meals together, going to movies, and so forth. This kind of non-crisis support goes such a long way in reducing stress and dysregulation that it may over time assist you to prevent crises.

Network Members

Here are some suggestions for potential members of your crisis network:

- Primary therapist

- Supportive/secondary therapist

- Group or ancillary therapist

- Case manager

- Physician

- Clergy

- Spiritual director

- Teacher/educator

- Twelve-step sponsor

- Friend from support group

- Coworker

- Your local crisis line and/or warm line

- Sibling

- Aunt/uncle

- Cousin

- Fellow student

- Other relatives

- Friends or acquaintances

Guidelines for Crisis Help via Phone

If you have a therapist who provides after-hours crisis coverage, arrange to call them first. If you don't hear from your therapist within one hour (or whatever the two of you agreed on), call your local city or county crisis line.

Tell the crisis-line worker whether or not you have a therapist, that you want to resolve the crisis, and that their support will be helpful. Accept the crisis worker's advice and instructions. If you don't know your local crisis-line number, call information, check your local directory, or ask your therapist.

If you're experiencing severely exacerbated symptoms of an existing mental disorder such as increased hallucinations, paranoia, or elevated mood as in the case of bipolar disorder, that may greatly compromise your safety or the safety of others, call your local crisis line, hospital, or 911 for an evaluation. You may require medication adjustments, immediate environmental support and safety, or perhaps a sub-acute/respite stay for stabilization. Some cities and provinces provide transportation if you're without your own or incapacitated.

If you have already injured yourself or are in a medical emergency, call 911 immediately.

If you're experiencing unmanageable distress and are contemplating suicide (thinking about ending your own life), and are in a situation where you might complete suicide, call 911 and/or follow protocols agreed upon between you and your therapist. Anyone without a therapist should call 911 under these circumstances.

Working with Crisis-Line Workers

I've been a crisis-line therapist, and I can tell you from experience that callers who were able take the following steps were more effective at reaching a fairly quick resolution about what to do. Following these guidelines won't ensure that your crisis will immediately abate, but it will increase your chances for effective outcomes that more closely match your goals for increased skillful living. Not every region will have the same resources, and not every region will have all kinds of crisis lines. You may need to call two counties over, or rely entirely on 911, or make alternate plans.

Whether the crisis line you call is staffed by mental health professionals or volunteers, the following guidelines can help you make the most effective use of your phone call.

Give all demographic information asked for

- Provide your name (that way, they don't have to call you "*you*")
- Your current physical address and location
- Home phone number, or if away from home current number at that time
- Social Security number
- Date of birth (there are age-related factors for health that are relevant in evaluation)
- Names of your primary care physician, psychiatrist, and therapist, if any
- Community mental health centers you may be affiliated with for case management
- Your insurance status (insured or uninsured), along with member number and HMO name (in case an evaluation is needed; this will speed the paperwork once you arrive to your crisis center or hospital)

- Provide information about prior hospitalizations

- Provide information on prior suicide attempts, or acts of self-harm and their outcomes

- Tell the crisis workers if you have any means of self-harm or suicide available

- Tell them any diagnosis you may carry (e.g., bipolar, PTSD, etc.)

- List any known allergies and/or medical conditions including issues of mobility (important if your crisis worker tries to provide you transportation)

Provide all relevant information about the crisis

- What precipitated the current crisis?

- What triggered your current emotions or feelings?

- Are you alone or with others?

- Whether or not you're currently injured

- If you're injured, tell them the nature of injury (laceration, overdose, asphyxiation)

- Is this a situation that can be resolved over the phone?

- Your opinion about whether you should go to a crisis center or hospital for evaluation

- Provide names of friends, family, or clergy as contacts as available

Accept help, coaching, suggestions, and instructions offered

- Be willing to go for an in-person evaluation

- Be willing to try to resolve the crisis in your environment

- Try suggestions as they are offered

- Don't "yes-but" the worker or pooh-pooh their ideas

- Don't reject their advice

- Don't judge the worker(s)

- Don't tell them they're stupid

- Don't expect the worker to take away your emotional pain

- Don't threaten the worker with suicide or self-harm

- Practice willingness over willfulness

- Participate fully in the experience

Acceptance Skills and Learning from Pain

What DBT calls *radical acceptance* is an inherent element of dialectical thinking and living. It is simply acknowledging what is before you, whether you like it or not. But acceptance isn't approval. That's a common misconception for clients who are new to DBT programs. Acceptance isn't simply putting up with misery. It is the starting point for profound change for you.

"Radical acceptance is letting go of fighting reality," writes Linehan (1993b, 102). What do we mean by "fighting reality"? An example might be the little girl who says that she will hold her breath until her parents or the world conforms to her wishes. It is both reality-rejecting and ineffective, because it does nothing but turn her face blue.

The word radical means fundamentally or foundationally. It comes from the Latin word *radix*, meaning "root." Radical acceptance is acceptance that comes from deep within you, acknowledging reality on its own terms without trying to reject it through willpower, or whining, or wallowing in misery. And, as Linehan puts it, "Acceptance is the only way out of hell" (1993b, 102). Acceptance lets you properly and accurately diagnose what is going on around you, and only when you accept in this way can you truly choose intentional and effective responses to your life. And even where certain factors can't be changed, acceptance allows you to more effectively tolerate the things that you can't change.

Dr. Viktor Frankl, a psychotherapist famous for his seminal work on Logotherapy entitled *Man's Search for Meaning*, gave a moving account of the power of acceptance as the ground for change and for building genuine hope. In his book, Frankl recounts his life as a Jew stripped of his privileged status as physician and university lecturer when the Nazis placed him in a concentration camp. In this camp he served as a physician to his fellow prisoners. He began to notice that among those who were dying and more frequently ill there was a prevalence of despair, hopelessness, and willfulness.

These sick and dying were generally people who were telling him and others about how awful it was to be in the camp, how God had abandoned them, and who ruminated on the terrible aspects of their situation. In contrast to this group, those that modeled health and required less medical attention were the prisoners who expressed hope, talked about the future beyond the camp, and who imagined reunions with loved ones or getting back to work. This second group had continued to engage in their lives and their existences such as they were, fully participating in those moments. They were willing; they said yes to their lives, and as Frankl notes, these were people who had stopped questioning life, asking what its meaning was, and instead began to respond to life, as though life had asked of them, "What will you make of me?"

I want to strongly reiterate the importance of regular practice and the idea of cultivating your practices so that they become integrated into your regular lifestyle from one day to the next. It isn't Pollyannaish to suggest that you can learn from your pain. Many people have suffered tremendously and come through it, extolling the hard truth that they gained something from their hardships. This may include insight, change of worldview, renewal of moral values, dedication to loved ones, spiritual discovery, and increased resilience. I believe the fact that so many people can learn and grow from their pain is evidence that you can too. It requires an openness of heart and mind to look at pain differently. Doing so is a skill to be learned, and to be learned it must be practiced.

Openness to the slings and arrows of life means letting pain be all that it is, without exacerbating it by judging it, or reacting to it by trying to reject its presence in your experience. This openness is what we have already talked about as willingness. Willingness to listen to pain to gain from it, to let pain become a mentor of sorts, letting it provide instruction and guidance.

I wish you the best possible outcome for all your efforts.

APPENDIX

The Emotion Thesaurus

The emotion thesaurus is adapted from *Skills Training Manual for Treating Borderline Personality Disorder* by Marsha Linehan (1993).

Love Words

The word *love* comes from the Indo-European *leubh-*. It is the root of the archaic English word *lief*, meaning dear, and the Latin word *libido* meaning "strong desire," indicating a connection between *love* and *attraction*. Other related words from the same root include *praise* and *belief*, which has an associated sense of "being pleased with."

- love
- adoration
- affection
- arousal
- attraction
- caring
- charmed

- compassion
- desire
- enchantment
- fondness
- infatuation
- kindness
- liking
- longing
- lust
- passion
- sentimentality
- sympathy
- tenderness
- warmth
- Other: _____

_____

_____

Joy Words

Some philosophers argue over whether or not joy is an emotion or an enduring sense of hopefulness and security. The word comes to English via Latin, from the same word from which we get our modern word *gaudy*. In Middle English it referred to an ornamental rosary bead. With respect to emotion, joy describes a state of great pleasure, happiness, or delight.

- joy
- amusement
- bliss
- cheerfulness
- contentment
- delight
- eagerness
- enjoyment

- enthrallment
- enthusiasm
- euphoria
- excitement
- exhilaration
- gladness
- glee
- happiness
- hope
- jubilation
- optimism
- pride
- rapture
- Other: _____

_____

_____

Interest Words

Interest comes the Latin verb *interesse* which means to "be between." Metaphorically the word meant "to be of concern," "be important," or "matter." From the fourteenth century on English adopted the word, eventually transforming it to *interest*. It was not until the end of the eighteenth century that it took its main sense of "curiosity."

- absorbed
- alluring
- attraction
- curiosity
- engaged
- engrossed
- enthrallment
- entice
- entranced
- fascination

- inquisitive

- interest

- intrusive

- probing

- studious

- temptation

- Other: _____

  _____

  _____

Anger Words

Anger may have come to Old English from Old Norse *angr* which may have been related to sorrow, but certainly once carried the meaning of pain, trouble, or affliction, much like a sore or inflammation. Anger is certainly an emotion of displeasure.

- anger

- aggravation

- agitation

- annoyance

- bitterness

- contempt

- cruelty

- destructiveness

- disgust

- dislike

- envy

- exasperation

- frustration

- grouchiness

- grumpiness

- hate

- hostility

- irritation

- jealousy

- outrage

- rage

- resentment

- wrath

- scorn

- Other: _____

_____

_____

Sadness Words

The word *sad* has its roots in the Indo-European words that culminated in our English words satisfy and *saturate* and originally meant "to have had enough." Eventually sad came to mean *weary* and then *unhappy*.

- sadness

- agony

- alienation

- anguish

- crushed

- defeat

- dejection

- despair

- disappointment

- discontent

- dismay

- displeasure

- distraught

- gloom

- grief

- hopeless

- hurt

- insecurity

- loneliness
- misery
- suffering
- Other: _____

_____

_____

Fear Words

Fear has its roots in the Old English *faer* and the Middle English *fer*, and has various connotations of dread, anxiety, terror, agitation, and alarm caused by the anticipation of danger.

- fear
- anxiety
- apprehension
- distress
- dread
- edginess
- fright
- horror
- hysteria
- jumpiness
- nervousness
- overwhelmed
- panic
- shock
- tenseness
- terror
- uneasiness
- worry
- Other: _____

_____

_____

Shame Words

Shame is a strong and painful form of guilt or sense of unworthiness, for doing wrong. The word, which comes from the Old and Middle English *sceamu,* is also directed to others, as in "to put someone to shame."

- shame
- contrition
- culpability
- discomposure
- embarrassment
- guilt
- humiliation
- insulted
- invalidation
- mortification
- regret
- remorse
- Other: _____

_____

_____

References

Dryden, Windy, and Raymond DiGiuseppe. 1990. *A Primer on Rational-Emotive Therapy.* Champaign, IL: Research Press.

Ellis, Albert. 1994. *Reason and Emotion in Psychotherapy.* New York: Birch Press Lane.

Goleman, Daniel. 1995. *Emotional Intelligence.* New York: Bantam.

Gottman, John, and Nan Silver. 1994. *Why Marriages Succeed or Fail.* New York: Fireside.

———. 1999. *The Seven Principles for Making Marriage Work.* New York: Three Rivers Press.

Greenberg, Leslie, and Susan M. Johnson. 1988. *Emotionally Focused Therapy for Couples.* New York: Guilford.

Greenberg, Leslie, and Sandra Paivio. 1997. *Working with Emotions in Psychotherapy.* New York: Guilford Press.

Kabat-Zinn, Jon. 1994. *Wherever You Go, There You Are.* New York: Hyperion.

Lazarus, Richard. 1991. *Emotion and Adaptation.* New York: Oxford University Press.

Linehan, Marsha. 1993a. *Cognitive-Behavioral Treatment of Borderline Personality Disorder* New York: Guilford.

———. 1993b. *Skills Training Manual for Treating Borderline Personality Disorder.* New York: Guilford.

Other Works Consulted

Gottman, John. 1997. *Raising an Emotionally Intelligent Child.* New York: Fireside.

Greenberg, Leslie, and J. Pascual-Leone. 1995. "A dialectical constructivist approach to experiential change." In Robert Neimeyer and Michael Mahoney, *Constructivism in Psychotherapy.* Washington, D.C.: APA Press.

Izard, Carroll. 1977. *Human Emotions.* New York: Plenum.

———. 1991. *The Psychology of Emotions.* New York: Plenum.

Jacobson, Edmund. 1967. *The Biology of Emotions.* Springfield, IL: Charles C. Thomas.

Kovecses, Zoltan. 1990. *Emotion Concepts.* New York: Springer-Verlag.

Lazarus, Richard, and Bernice Lazarus. 1994. *Passion and Reason: Making Sense of Our Emotions.* Washington, D.C.: APA Press.

Niedenthal, Paula, and Shinobu Kitayama, eds. 1994. *The Heart's Eye: Emotional Influence in Perception and Attention.* San Diego: Academic Press.

Strongman, Ken. 1996. *The Psychology of Emotion: Theories of Emotion in Perspective.* New York: John Wiley.

Tomkins, Silvan, and Carroll Izard, eds. 1965. *Affect, Cognition, and Personality* (4th ed.). New York: Springer Publishing.

Traue, Harald, and James Pennebaker, eds. 1993. *Emotion, Inhibition, and Health.* Göttingen, Germany: Hogrefe & Huber.

Some Other
New Harbinger Titles

Angry All the Time, Item 3929 $13.95

Handbook of Clinical Psychopharmacology for Therapists, 4th edition, Item 3996 $55.95

Writing For Emotional Balance, Item 3821 $14.95

Surviving Your Borderline Parent, Item 3287 $14.95

When Anger Hurts, 2nd edition, Item 3449 $16.95

Calming Your Anxious Mind, Item 3384 $12.95

Ending the Depression Cycle, Item 3333 $17.95

Your Surviving Spirit, Item 3570 $18.95

Coping with Anxiety, Item 3201 $10.95

The Agoraphobia Workbook, Item 3236 $19.95

Loving the Self-Absorbed, Item 3546 $14.95

Transforming Anger, Item 352X $10.95

Don't Let Your Emotions Run Your Life, Item 3090 $17.95

Why Can't I Ever Be Good Enough, Item 3147 $13.95

Your Depression Map, Item 3007 $19.95

Successful Problem Solving, Item 3023 $17.95

Working with the Self-Absorbed, Item 2922 $14.95

The Procrastination Workbook, Item 2957 $17.95

Coping with Uncertainty, Item 2965 $11.95

The BDD Workbook, Item 2930 $18.95

You, Your Relationship, and Your ADD, Item 299X $17.95

The Stop Walking on Eggshells Workbook, Item 2760 $18.95

Conquer Your Critical Inner Voice, Item 2876 $15.95

The PTSD Workbook, Item 2825 $17.95

Hypnotize Yourself Out of Pain Now!, Item 2809 $14.95

The Depression Workbook, 2nd edition, Item 268X $19.95

Beating the Senior Blues, Item 2728 $17.95

Shared Confinement, Item 2663 $15.95

Getting Your Life Back Together When You Have Schizophrenia, Item 2736 $14.95

Do-It-Yourself Eye Movement Technique for Emotional Healing, Item 2566 $13.95

Call **toll free, 1-800-748-6273,** or log on to our online bookstore at **www.newharbinger.com** to order. Have your Visa or Mastercard number ready. Or send a check for the titles you want to New Harbinger Publications, Inc., 5674 Shattuck Ave., Oakland, CA 94609. Include $4.50 for the first book and 75¢ for each additional book, to cover shipping and handling. (California residents please include appropriate sales tax.) Allow two to five weeks for delivery.

Prices subject to change without notice.